AF506961

Bare Witness II:

Growing Beyond Grief

Krystal Carr

Bare Witness II: Growing Beyond Grief

Copyright © 2022 by Krystal Carr

All rights reserved. No part of this book may be reproduced or transmitted in any form or by any means without written permission from the author.

ISBN (979-8-9858809-4-6)

Disclaimer: The following versions of the Bible may have been referenced: New International Version (NIV), King James Version (KJV), New Living Translation (NLT), English Standard Version (ESV), New King James (NKJV), New International Reader's Version (NIRV), Christian Standard Bible (CSB), Common English Bible (CEB), The Message (MSG).

MTE Publishing — mtepublishing.com

Dedication

"Bare Witness II," is lovingly dedicated to my amazing husband, beautiful children & grandchildren, and my late beloved mother.

My Darling Vincent, the love and compassion that you have shown me throughout our relationship is priceless. To me, you are the perfect example of how Christ loved HIS church and gave HIMSELF for it. I love you with everything in me.

Keyana, I don't think you realize how strong you actually are. You are the kindest, most gentle soul I've ever known. I am proud to call you daughter. Keep living life to the fullest, even when you think it's too full just make more room. You are the brightest light, keep shining no matter how dark you may think it gets. I love you so much sugar, you are your mother's daughter! And to my beautiful grandchildren, Hayden and Haelyn, Mia loves you!

Keiton, or shall I say *It's Kei*, you are an absolutely amazing young man. Life has handed you some things that you did not deserve, yet you handled them with grace and love. You did not let those situations and circumstances change your heart and if it did change, it only got bigger. I now know for sure you are a momma's boy, even if you won't admit it. Continue to let your creativity guide you, perfect your gift and let it make room for you. Don't EVER settle for less than the best for yourself. Find out what you want and who you want to be and go full force towards your vision. You can have whatever you like! I Love the man that you are and the even bigger man that you are becoming.

Dewayne, it's been four long years since I've heard your voice, seen your face, and been graced with your beautiful smile… in real time. I miss you more than words can express and at times more than my heart can bear. Every silent tear I cry screams "I love you and I miss you." Thank you for the seventeen beautiful years that you spent with me.

Even though it seemed so short, I will remember for a lifetime. I Love you eternally, but… I'm still gonna whoop you ass when I see you!

Ma, I know we haven't always seen eye to eye, but I love you unconditionally. Over the years we exchanged words that hadn't always been pleasant. Nevertheless, on the day of April 8 our hearts were completely connected as our last words to each other were "I love you" and "I love you more". Thank you for being the doorway into life's entrance. It ain't always been a bed of roses, but I'm making the most of it. It's been a year since you left us, and it still seems surreal. I miss your laughter and I miss your smile. I'm glad you're not in any more pain, but I wish it could have ended another way. At *attention*, you fought a good fight soldier, now be *at ease* and take your rest! I love you, always & forever.

Table of Contents

Introduction:

Articulating Grief

I tried intensely to articulate what grief is. I tried to propose a literal definition. However, I came face to face with the horrid reality that there is not nor will there ever be a sustained term for what grief really is. Today, as I write this, I feel as though I have temporarily accepted the reality of my baby boy being gone *forever*. Simultaneously, the word "forever" just hit me like a semitruck, and I am now shedding tears as if April 28th, 2018, is happening now. In my mind *it is*. Fortunately, I understand the grief that attempts to paralyze me is the very entity that also compels and *propels* me to *move from here*… Dewayne, I will see you again in the ever after. Mrs. Thomas, I will never BE you again… you have been dismissed! Hello, Ms. Carr it is nice to make your acquaintance again… this time, "our love" won't die!

Grief, your intrusive entry into my life caused me to fall and fly, sink, and swim, but more importantly, grab my reality, confront it, and grow! The grief within my life is continual. It is not represented as a death, but it is the unforeseen beginning of a necessary part of my intentional progression. I don't like this. As a matter of fact, I despise it. Grief, I would make a bold attempt to kick your ass if you were a person! Unfortunately, you're not, so I simply ride your waves as they come. Sometimes I get wiped out, and other times I ride it out, but in everything you've thrown at me and nonchalantly handed to me, I refuse to stop growing.

Chapter 1

A Blind Date with Grief

Grief… What does *it* mean to you? Take a second to mull that over. Whenever the word "grief" is heard, our minds automatically parallel the term with death. This is feasible because death is the most grievous thing that one can and will experience in this life. The Bible even calls it our "ultimate enemy." The all-encompassing meaning across references defines grief as "deep sorrow," especially caused by someone's death. Even though this is the most prominent association, grief's attachment is rooted in more than death, and having experienced many avenues of grief I can attest to the indescribable impact that it leaves in different areas of our lives. I have come to know that it is much more than just a deep sadness. Grief can summatively and cohesively be described as deep sadness, sorrow, trouble, or annoyance associated with a significant or sudden loss. This definition is practical, but not exhaustive. It attempts to give a concrete meaning to the word, but it does not explicitly describe the magnitude of what it is and what it does to those who experience it. Grief is a whole body, it has a whole mind, and it is wholly spiritual; death consummated my relationship with Grief, and I understood that the effect of having this forced relationship with him would possibly last forever.

Grief and I have made many acquaintances. We've met here and there on occasions, just as he has visited most of you reading this book. I have learned how to ignore his presence and carry on as if he were not there at all. I've suffered many significant emotional losses in my life which would bring about the presence of grief… the loss of relationships, the loss of loved ones (aunts, uncles, cousins, grandparents), loss of material things (houses, cars, money,) the list goes on. However, I didn't have the time, patience, or strength to establish a relationship with Grief in order to learn the purpose of his presence. I practiced the art of pain avoidance at all costs, as most of us do. We are readily equipped to assign a scripture, an old wives' tale, or a misquoted bible referenced colloquialism to our situation to soothe the pain as if this was some topical solution that we could apply for temporary surface relief.

How many of you or your family members have had one basic, end-all-be-all solution used as a remedy for all maladies? I once watched a television series called "Everybody Hates Chris" and the mom's drug of choice for any ailment was Robitussin. The kids would get hurt, "Ouch, I burned my finger," and she would say "Let me see… Oh, take some Robitussin." In one instance, in response to a broken tooth, Mom's save the day response was "I'll go get the Robitussin." Another time, "Mom, Chris just got hit by a car," followed by Mom's urgent response "Oh my God, I'll go get the Robitussin."

As funny as this may seem, when we consider how often we exercise this concept and treat our ill health with "Robitussin" instead of properly assessing the situation and finding out what it is that we really need for real healing to occur, it's shameful to admit and almost impossible to accept the negligence on our part.

Unfortunately, I was the one who operated in this manner for forty years. Saved, sanctified, and filled with the Holy Ghost, but still in the wilderness and still using "Robitussin!" Until one day, something happened in my life that shook the very foundations of my world. On April 28, 2018, I awoke like any other day, I had an event to decorate and my son, Dewayne, helped me prepare for it the night before. I got dressed and went to get him to help me load the truck. I went to his room first, I didn't find him there… and usually, if he was not in his room he would sleep in his brother's room on the couch. So, I went from one room to the next. As I pushed open the door, expecting to find my son laid out on the couch, he was not there either. Immediately, my heart sank to the bottom of my feet, and I belted out "Where is DEWAYNE?" I walked from the hallway, peered at the front door, and noticed that it was unlocked. "Oh, he must have gone for a walk," I said while trying to settle my nerves. I approached the front door, opened it, and looked to my right towards the road to see if I saw him coming back or going for a walk. When I didn't see him, I prepared my lungs to let out a yell for him, and before I could let it go, I looked to my left and in the corner of the yard, I saw him lying on top of his comforter on the ground. I shook my head and wondered, "Why is that boy sleeping outside?" As I looked again, I noticed that there was something protruding from his chest and immediately, I felt my spirit leave my body. Consequently, I remember everything that happened next because it occurred in slow motion. All I could say was no, no, no, no, no. I went over to my son and removed this thing that was hurting him and called frantically for him to get up, slapping his face to wake him up. I hollered for my then-husband, he called 911 and I called my pastors. This enemy called Death had shown up to my front door and I was determined he wouldn't win *that day*. I called in the reinforcers to touch and agree with me in prayer for the power of resurrection. I went back over to my son, and I put my hands in his hand like Elijah was over that girl, and I began to pray, I prayed over him, and my pastors prayed over the phone. As I prayed, I felt a hand on my shoulder and I heard audibly, "He made his choice and I have to honor it." I yelled within myself, "I don't like his choice!"

By then the ambulance showed up and I had to move to let them do their job, to bring him back. They were moving very slowly, when they got there, I knew that it was over, but I still refused to accept it. The one guy grabbed the sheet, he saw me watching him closely, he tried to hide it behind him. I looked at him and said very sternly, "Don't you put that on him!" As soon as I turned my head, he covered him with the sheet, and I ran over and snatched it off and screamed

"I told you not to put that on him!" In that moment and the days that followed, my mind was in a true state of denial. I spent weeks on the couch trying to walk through what I thought were his last steps. I attempted to relive *that day* so I would be there to stop it. I spent weeks trying to *undo it.* At that point, I was literally on the verge of a nervous breakdown, and I didn't even know it.

What some people viewed as strength was actually suppression. I was not dealing with this at all. I did not want to feel this pain, so I completely disconnected from it and with it. How is that possible you ask? This pain was like NO other. I've experienced pithy sessions about Grief through the death of close loved ones before; however, I never had an established relationship with him to know what he was really about. But something about this experience was different and outweighed every adverse experience in my life. Not only had Grief found a lodging place but he brought his relative, Trauma, to be his roommate. During the course of a few weeks, I had literal out-of-body experiences. I was here, but I wasn't here. I asked the questions: WHY? WHY is this happening to me? Am I a horrible mother? What did I miss? How did I miss it? Was I too busy? Should I have paid more attention? Did I do everything that I could have? Did I do everything that I should have?

I was at a total loss. I was truly at the end of myself. There was nothing I could do in my own strength that could help me through this. Certainly not the "Robitussin Remedy." I needed GOD and I needed HIM right away. Not the God of my mother, not the God of my father, or grandparents, but I needed HIM in a whole new way for me.

With an eerie and brooding existence, these characters Grief and Trauma invaded my space, and this time, there was no ignoring their presence. There was an immediate marriage to the both of them, a lifetime commitment, a covenant relationship. In this established relationship, I had to learn of them, learn of me, and finally learn more from HIM (GOD). I knew that if I didn't learn how to cope and how to manage this, I too would be absent from the body and present with the LORD. So, the journey of my rediscovery began.

First, I had to understand and know that we are spiritual beings having a natural experience. With that being said, I knew that I had to understand that which was natural to get an inkling of an understanding of the spiritual and how they coexist... I recognized that I was not going through this process "correctly" and in all honesty, I was not going through *it* at all. In my quest for healing, I began to examine my inner-self and search for resources to help me through this tremendously weighty process. In my discovery, some experts say that grief can be summed up in five stages. Listed below are the referenced stages of grief and my perceived processes according to each stage.

1.   **Denial** – The honeymoon phase of grief. It is very common for people to try and initially

deny the event in order to subconsciously avoid sadness or the thought of pending mental struggles. People in denial often withdraw from their normal social behavior and become isolated. Denial has no set time frame or may never be felt at all. "This is not my life, it's just a horrible dream that I will soon awake from."

2.   **Anger** – The heated phase of grief. People that are grieving often become upset with the person or situation that placed them with Grief. *"Here I am, a child of the MOST-HIGH GOD, doing everything I knew to do, yet this is my lot... go figure. Hey Job, I heard you say, "Thou you slay me yet will I trust you." HOW???? And WHY in the HELL would you or could you trust after all the SHIT you've been through? God specifically handed you to SATAN and you still trust HIM? Hey David, I heard you singing "the LORD is my SHEPHERD, and I will not lack anything." You*

also said in that same song that death was just a shadow. Then, what the F#CK is this DAVID. This for damn sure looks like LACK and DEATH at the same damn time... this AIN'T a shadow! I wanna know how you came to **this** *conclusion.* But… I never really blamed God.

3.   **Bargaining** – The compromising phase of grief. I pleaded, begged, and implored God, "PLEASE, just let me redo *that day*! That is all I want, make me a time-traveler, and permit time to stand still while allowing me to move - and DO the readjustments! Dewayne will be here with me as usual! This sounds like a great plan to me, alright God?" Wishful, hurtful, reality slapping me in the face even as I try to sleep. Please don't wake me. Let me dream because Dewayne is there.

4.   **Depression** – The "silent treatment" phase of grief. Sleep, silence, alone, stuck, repeat. Sleep, silence, alone, stuck, repeat. Nothingness.

There was nothing in it. Emptiness. What could've been said to change reality? Nothing. Silence. Let me just be, the monotony might kill me… but I won't HEAR the pain!

5. **Acceptance** – The maturing phase of grief. At this point, I am still trying to understand the "who, what, when, where, why, and how" of Dewayne's ending and how his ending connects to my beginning. How can I, the one who birthed him, also be the one who buried him and at the same time understand the reasons. Acceptance, where are you? Grief is still standing in your place; I see him, feel him, hear him, smell him, taste him. Yet I am still working to truly know him despite not wanting him… Why? I believe GOD had a proposal of purpose through the connection.

I said, "This isn't happening," (denial). I screamed, "WHY IS THIS HAPPENING?" (anger). I bartered "Let's do this over, so I can stop it" (bargaining). I cried "Well, I will just sleep it off" (depression). Finally, I stood still and said, "What now?" (acceptance - I don't know yet.). Somehow this process felt incomplete, there were some things that I was experiencing that didn't fit into any of these categories. These stages did not seem to suit my overall situation, but I attempted to define this mystery with the information that had been presented until I discovered more. I continued to search for additional methods to heal. Weeks after the death of my son, one of my very good friends invited me to join a support group at her church. She agreed to accompany me on these days as a resource of support. This grief group's mission was to offer an outlet to those dealing with grief. We would sit in a circle, and everyone would share their stories of grief over the loss of a loved one. Thirteen weeks of talking about my grief and experiences seemed to offer very little sense of relief. Surely, an attempt was made to carve out a path on the road to recovery, but even in that I recognized the need for more.

I was referred to a trauma therapist and this was an experience in itself. During my first appointment, conversation ensued as to the circumstances that warranted this meeting. She had an idea, as the person that referred me gave insight into my ordeal. She inquired about the situation and in preparation and anticipation for what she was about to hear, she gathered her pen and pad to take notes.

"So, tell me what brings you here today," she prompted.

"Well," then I go into my story. She started out writing the notes, then she caught a glance at me as she looked up from her paper. She subtly moved her notes to the side and vehemently studied my facial expressions and emotional affect. After I finished the story, I noticed that she had a perplexed look on her face.

She said, "I see why you were referred to me, and here's why. When you said that story it was as if you were going to the grocery store and reading off a grocery list. Monotone, emotionless, blank. You are not dealing with this. You're not allowing yourself to feel it, and if you continue like this you're going to end up in a strait jacket or worse." She proceeded to educate me on the brain and the effects of trauma and my responses to trauma. She then developed a treatment plan that was specific to my case. When I went for the first treatment session, I didn't know what to expect. There were all types of gadgets and apparatus in the room. How many of you have seen the movie "Get Out"? (An excellent movie if you get a chance to see it, you should.) I liken my experience to the particular scene in which the guy was hypnotized and in his state of hypnosis, the hypnotist sent him to the sunken place in his mind where he couldn't function properly. The thing that would make them snap out of this debilitated state of mind was the flash of a camera. With this scene stuck in my head, I brought my daughter with me, just in case the therapist tried to send me to the sunken place, and I needed my daughter to utilize the camera flash to bring me back. The treatment plan that was implemented caused my brain to be unlocked and allowed me to become appropriately acquainted with Grief. She used something similar to what we have seen on TV as hypnosis, but it wasn't that. I didn't get sleepy, I wasn't incoherent, she didn't tell me to bark like a dog. None of that, but she exercised my brain waves. She explained the after-effects of the procedures, but I was very skeptical. I'm like, "I have a strong mind lady, this stuff is not going to work on me!" But let me tell you that it did. Every emotion that I tried to suppress came in like a flood and I couldn't stop it, I had to let it happen. That is when the healing process began; however, I didn't know just how long the journey would be.

I shared that part of my experience to interject that too many of us have been exposed to and extricated through many difficult situations. Although we are resilient and our survival skills are through the roof, everything becomes about survival, but there are times when it is necessary to learn another mindset and attain additional skill sets. There are a plethora of resources and services that we can and should utilize in order to help us move through the difficult processes in life. Yes, we depend on God. Yes, we can do all things through Christ who strengthens us, but the reality is "we [His people] perish for lack of knowledge or in ignorance. It is not His will that we remain in ignorance. In all our getting we should get a full understanding of who we are, what we are, and whose we are. Don't let the stigma people place on counseling, therapy, or things of that nature cause you to be stifled in your healing. As I mentioned before, we are spiritual beings having a natural experience, right? We must speak to our entire existence. We must ensure that we are doing everything necessary to take care of this body (naturally) which is the temple of the Lord, and the Holy Spirit will handle the spiritual part as long as we are feeding on the WORD.

Dewayne's completed suicide forced me to stop surviving, to stop throwing scriptures and colloquialisms at situations, and to stop hiding behind a mask of "perceived strength." It was high time that I "died." I'm not talking in a literal sense, although there were several times that I actually wanted *death* to become my reality. It was time for me to be in that place where my survival skills alone could not carry me through. There was no fake it til you make it; no putting makeup on and dressing it up to look nice, and no perfect, put-together, pretty words that were enough to get me through. I needed rescuing. I needed the instruction and guidance from God, and I was open to whatever He told me to do. I was in no position to question Him about his methods. I had to rely totally on Him if I were going to make it out of this.

I have learned more about myself and even more about God while being with Grief. Nothing I've been through up until this point has weighed more heavily on me; it caused a complete paradigm shift. A shift in the way I think, a shift in the way I view things, a shift in the way I respond to things, a complete and total shift. This thing, this relationship with Grief, caused me to become a new creature. No longer a creature of habit. The Bible says it best "In Christ, I become a new creature and old things have passed away and behold all things become new" (2 Corinthians 5:17). Some of us are offended by pain, we think we don't deserve it because we are a friend of God, and our friends don't let dreadful things happen to us. But some things we go through are not happening to us but are happening for us to develop something greater in us. Most of the time the pain is necessary as it is an internal issue that needs to be dealt with concerning us. More often than not, we don't want to deal with ourselves. We'd rather deal with other people and let them know their issues. We pay attention to their speck while our beam continues to impale our vision and causes us to remain complacent. Forward movement is impossible when your vision is obstructed; Proverbs 29:18-19, 21 says "Where there is no vision, the people perish: but he that keepeth the law, happy is he. A servant will not be corrected by words: for though he understands he will not answer... He that delicately bringeth up his servant from a child shall have him become his son at the length."

The things that God uses to develop us makes no good earthly sense, as it is not supposed to, 1 Corinthians 1:27 declares "But God, hath chosen the foolish things of the world to confound the wise; and God hath chosen the weak things of the world to confound the things which are mighty." Another translation reads "God chose things the world considers foolish in order to shame those who think they are wise. And he chose things that are powerless to shame those that are powerful." Just when you think you have acquired knowledge, is when you find out you haven't even scratched the surface of knowing. I've learned through this process that there are so many facets to God. There are so many levels and although He is not the source of our pain, He uses our pain to process and develop us if we allow Him to do that. His entire M.O. (modus operandi) is to move us from servant to son. The Bible is filled with examples of adversities and painful situations and circumstances, but through those trials' men and women experienced Victory when they walked hand and hand with God. We cannot experience a victory if we give up, avoid the process, and waste our pain. That is what makes us stronger. Not physically stronger, but stronger in our Faith. When we go through things and come out on the other side, that becomes a reference point or an altar that we can build at that specific place in our lives and say… I call this place BETHEL for surely the Lord was in this place and I did not know it. (Genesis 28:19)

Chapter 2

Grief What... Grief Who?

Grief, who are you? Who let you in? Grief, what are you? Are you a consequence of my sin? When will you leave? Will you ever go away? Why are you here? Did you come to stay? How did you get here? Who led you to me? Why won't you go? Why won't you flee? Do you have a reason? Do you have a rhyme? To invade my space. To steal my time. Do you have any answers to give? If not, please go and just let me live.

Grief is described in many different ways. It could be summed up simplistically as deep sorrow or in its complexity as a multifaceted response to loss, particularly to the loss of someone or something that has died, to which a bond or affection was formed. Although conventionally focused on the emotional response to loss, it also has physical, cognitive, behavioral, social, cultural, spiritual, and philosophical dimensions. The answer to that question was so eloquently stated and seemed to possess educationally relevant verbiage, but that is not really the answer that is acceptable to assist me in my relationship with grief. In answering the question, I really want to know, I need to confront grief head-on. Grief, who are you? Where did you come from? Who sent you? Why are you here? What purpose do you serve?

Previously Grief and I had several brief encounters, A few flings, and a couple one-night stands, but on April 28, 2018, we exchanged nuptials and were pronounced partners for life. This union was so unexpected. Unlike my previous marriages, Grief held me at gunpoint and forced me into submission. As a matter of fact, I was in an unconscious state during the ceremony as if I were under the influence of a date rape drug, in a stupor. On the day I discovered and approached my son's lifeless body lying atop his bed comforter with a knife impaled in his chest, it was like my spirit had left my body. As if I entered into a time warp of another dimension. Everything became cloudy and confusing and things around me began to move at an exponential speed while my mind and body experienced a type of paralysis. Sights and sounds of sirens and flashing lights could be seen and heard far off. Where are they off to? What tragedy awaits them? Well, this day, it was my house. As the first responders arrived, they knew upon approach that my son had already departed. As protocol demanded, they hooked him up to a defibrillator to try to detect a heartbeat or faint pulse. I stood and watched intently with arms folded as they attempted to find any signs of life.

I saw one EMT move toward the truck, grab a white sheet, and put it behind his back as he looked over at me. In my anger and disbelief, I yelled "Don't you put that on him!" He didn't as long as I was looking at him, but as soon as I turned my head, he quickly put the sheet over him. I screamed "I told you not to put that on him!" I ran over and snatched it off. I was met by an officer who grabbed me and said, "Ma'am you can't do that."

Then started the investigation… What? I'm being investigated. Yellow tape surrounded the perimeter of the house. I was inundated with questions. Photographs were taken of the front and back of my hands. Knowing this was the proper protocol that they had to follow didn't ease the shock and disbelief of this moment that I was in… It intensified the trauma. By this time, my pastors were on their way. I called my mother, on the phone I explained to her that I needed her and not to ask any questions, just come. And what was the first thing she did… yep, you guessed it she asked a goddamn question… I hung up the phone. Then I called Dewayne's dad and aunt to briefly tell them what happened. I had to make the dreaded call to my daughter. Of course, I didn't tell her what happened over the phone, I just told her that she needed to get to the house, I tried to remain as calm as possible so she would not panic. I only called specific family members and friends at this time; however, word travels fast and before I knew it the whole "G" clan swarmed my house. There were whispers and speculations of what they thought happened. It's amazing how quickly people can conjure up a story without knowing any information. The blame was shifted to my husband at the time. Conversations and whispers, some people were recording and posting this grievous moment on Facebook, really people? The lies and slander had started before the investigation was over. Family members were scattered saying, "I don't believe he did this to himself; he doesn't know anything about that." Consequently, these were family members that didn't really know my son. Sure, they did a few drive-by encounters, but they only knew him associatively but not enough to speak on anything about him intimately. Dramatic antics from "those" family members continued as I fought to keep my mind and heart stable. I couldn't believe this was happening to me. I not only had to deal with the shock and pain of losing my son, but also the trauma caused by finding him, and to top it off to deal with the emotional trauma that came with the investigation and from members of the family. Although surrounded by family and friends, I was all alone. Alone in my feelings. Alone with a broken heart. Alone with Grief. It was a day I will never forget, but it is a day that I wish I did not have to commit to memory. I hoped this was a terrible nightmare from which I would soon wake up; nonetheless, nearly two years later… I am still asleep.

Phase 1: Shock

Shock- *a sudden upsetting or surprising event or experience causing sudden emotional stress often marked by cold, pallid skin, irregular breathing, rapid pulse, and dilated pupils.*

The investigation was over. The conclusion: a single, self-inflicted stab wound to the chest. Dewayne's body was placed on a cold, hard, steel gurney. We looked at him one last time before he was removed and transported in the frigidly confined steel walls of the medical examiner's van. The mood was somber, shocking, and eerily grievous. I couldn't feel my body. I had no idea how I was still moving or breathing. My eight senses had become debilitated. At this point, my reactions were either hyper-responsive (overreacted) or hypo-responsive (under reacted). As the people cleared, the fog thickened.

In my debilitated state of mind and paralysis due to the shocking nature of the situation, I suddenly remembered that I had a party to decorate, so I snapped into action and busied myself with work. I packed the truck and hurried to the park. Some friends joined me as I tried to make something pretty out of this ugly situation. No matter how I tried to fix it up, nothing worked. This was true for the decorations and the situation… As this visual reel continued to replay in my head like the threads of a film strip through a projector, I wanted so badly to rewrite the ending of this tragic story, but I couldn't… I've had to face the reality of it all. It's neither a sweet dream nor a beautiful nightmare… just an a completely fucked up reality!

Chapter 3

Grief's Proposal

Some people may describe their Grief as being punctuated by sighs, tears, and sometimes groans. I wish I knew him like that. That would be considered healthy, like a great marriage. One that has ups and downs, but growth happens through those tough moments when love overrides, overrules, and conquers all. Grief, as I knew him, was savage. My Grief was emphasized by silent screams, invisible uncontrollable tears, and internal tantrums. He brought the cyclic pain of a toxic relationship, consistently unpleasant and draining like an abusive spouse whose insecurities cause a spiraling of violent rage. He didn't care who was around, he acted out when he wanted, where he wanted, just because he wanted. When he had a point to prove, he did it with force without regard for innocent bystanders.

My reactions to him were at best unrealistic. I made excuses for him. Avoiding eye contact with him, I pretended that he was not there. I busied myself so that I did not have to think about the hell that I'd go through *with him*. At a glance, no one could fathom the measure of pain and anguish I experienced. Facial expressions never gave way to the excruciating discomfort of circumstantial evidence intently concealed by a stupefied demeanor.

Death gave Grief direct access to my life and unapologetically Grief came in and made himself comfortable. He invaded my space… emotionally, mentally, physically, and spiritually. Dewayne's absence created an immense vacancy and Grief saw this as a perfect opportunity to occupy. It was an unusual, yet common seduction. He recognized my emotional pain, brokenness, and vulnerability and regarded me as the perfect prey. When at my lowest ebb, he pounced on my weakness and before I even knew what hit me, I was captured in his entanglement. It was a traditional Kyrgyzstan marriage by abduction. A practice in which one is sought out, abducted, enslaved, raped, then forced into marriage. Our relationship paralyzed me… it tried to keep me in a state of helplessness and hopelessness. Grief was relentless. This was in fact the ultimate abusive relationship. He controlled every move I made. Everywhere I went he tagged along, keeping me in check making sure that there wouldn't be any joyous moments. He often isolated me from family and friends keeping me confined all to himself. He was smothering. Even as I slept, he would snuggle in close, hold me tight, and remind me of the day we met. As long as he had me in his clutches, I was powerless, subjected to his unjust demands as if I was under a spell. If he said, "Stay in bed all day," I did. If he said, "Don't eat today," I didn't. Those stolen moments of light that caused me to smile would instantly be dimmed, as Grief's subtle whispers evoked feelings of guilt, shame, and despair. In those rushed escapes he sought me out, stopped me in my tracks, then dragged me back into that same merciless domicile I attempted to flee.

I felt like I was living in a continual nightmare. However, the reality of Grief, forcing himself into my life always took me back to *that* day… the day my Joy, said "See you later," and Grief mockingly announced, "Honey, I am home!" I tried to ignore him like I did most things in my life during this time, but Grief never allowed me to just be. I flaunted this fake display of supernatural strength because I believed I had to. If anyone found out that Grief was really kicking my ass, I would no longer be hidden from my shame! People would really know how *guilty* I felt, and how much I had taken the blame, and I couldn't face this. More importantly, I didn't want to.

Phase 2: Denial

Denial- the action of declaring something to be untrue.

This can't be my life was the record that spun on the turntable in my mind. The strings, chords, percussion, and horns shrieked continuously as the wrestling match between my soul and spirit battled for supremacy. Through the deafening commotion amidst this battle, I tried to discover ways to put an end to this unfair fight. The first unrealistic tactic was to trick my mind into believing that this thing didn't really happen. "Dewayne did say he was going to Alaska," I would say to myself. I remember the conversation that he and his brother, Keiton, had about the anticipated move. (TRVLL.LIFE3 = Dewayne; ME = Keiton)

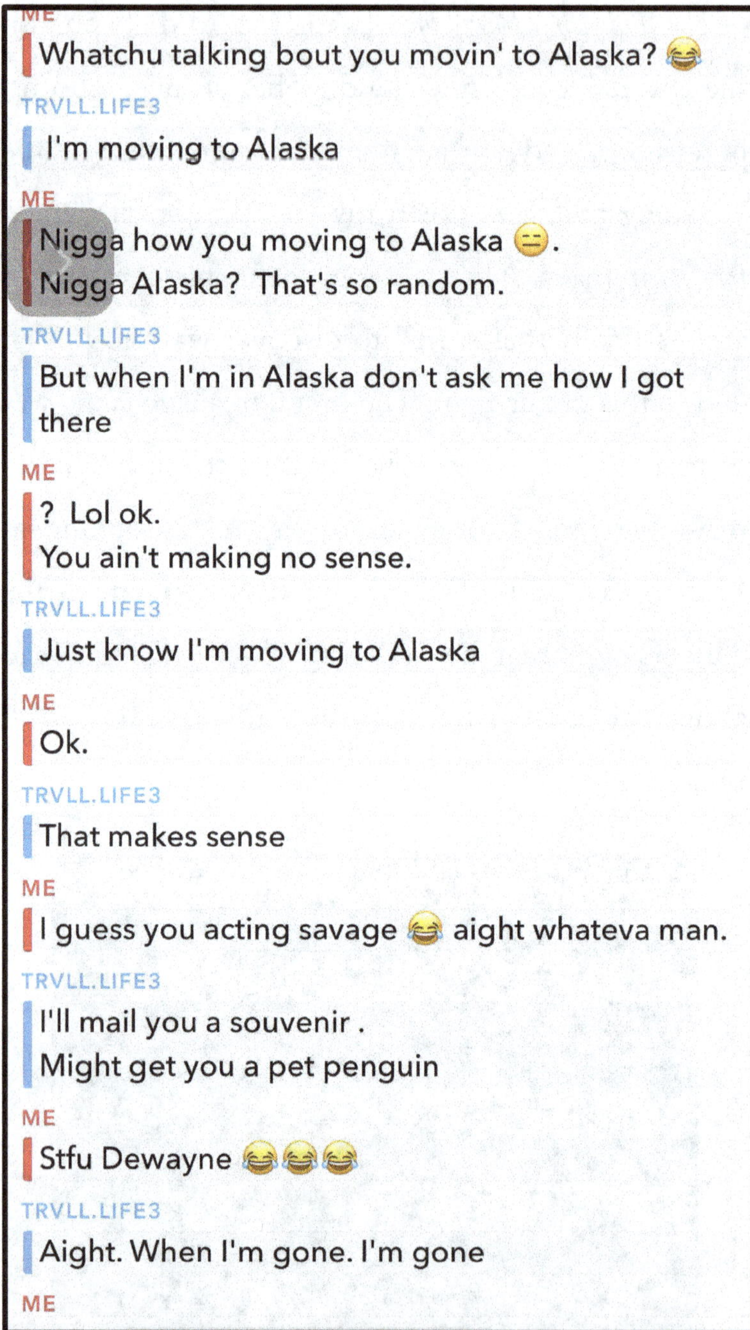

ME
Whatchu talking bout you movin' to Alaska? 😂

TRVLL.LIFE3
I'm moving to Alaska

ME
Nigga how you moving to Alaska 😑.
Nigga Alaska? That's so random.

TRVLL.LIFE3
But when I'm in Alaska don't ask me how I got
there

ME
? Lol ok.
You ain't making no sense.

TRVLL.LIFE3
Just know I'm moving to Alaska

ME
Ok.

TRVLL.LIFE3
That makes sense

ME
I guess you acting savage 😂 aight whateva man.

TRVLL.LIFE3
I'll mail you a souvenir .
Might get you a pet penguin

ME
Stfu Dewayne 😂😂😂

TRVLL.LIFE3
Aight. When I'm gone. I'm gone

ME

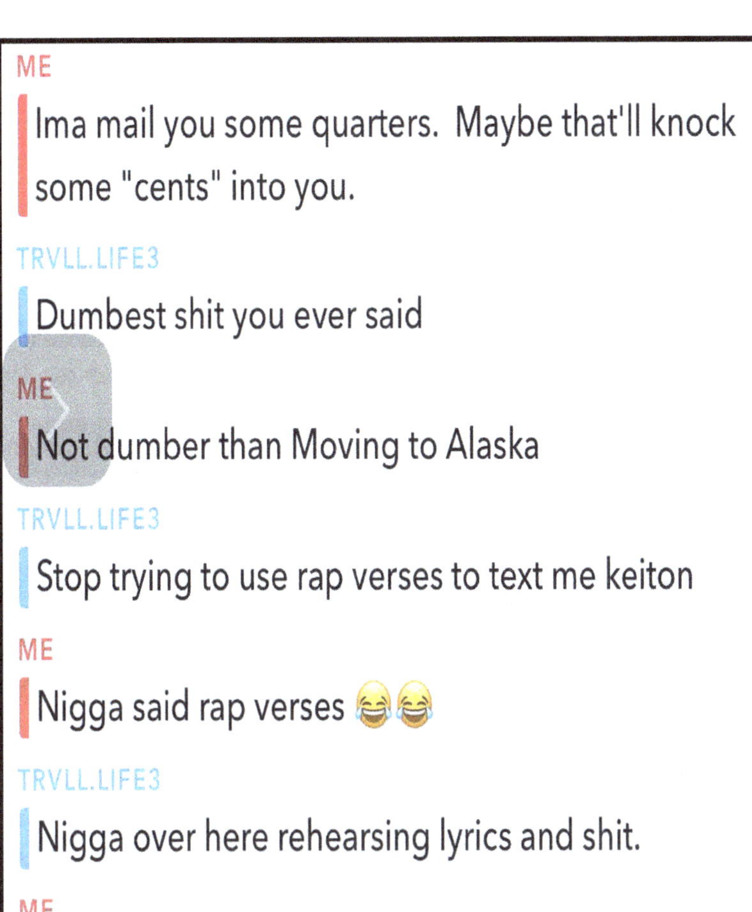

(Please excuse the teenage vernacular)

Although revisiting the dialogue between my sons was quite entertaining, it wasn't enough to dismiss the actual occurrence. The next strategy was to observe how others grieved with similar tragedies. My go-to resource was the movie entitled, *The Shack*. This movie is a Christian-based film in which a family searched for answers after the abduction and murder of their youngest daughter. I vehemently studied the way in which they dealt with Grief and with God and HE with them.

Photo with William P. Young, author of The Shack.

I spent days on the couch watching this movie searching for a conclusion to this matter, and still none was found to fully assuage my pain. I was completely and utterly enveloped in the initial onset of Grief. If that wasn't enough, the next plan was so far beyond reality and rational thinking that it would literally take a well-thought-out treatment program to bring me back from that. I had a plan to return to that night before and stop him. I thought if I had just stayed and slept on the couch… I would have heard him plundering around the kitchen as he chose the weapon of his demise. I would have noticed something was off when he draped himself in his bed comforter and made his way into the parlor. I would have heard the creaking of the front door as he attempted to go outside. I didn't get a chance to do any of these things before, but I'm going to redeem the time and do it over. Night after night I positioned myself on the couch and waited into the wee hours of the night. If I so happened to fall asleep, I would icily awaken to make sure that I didn't miss it this time.

One particular night, I was surprised at what I experienced. In one of my many attempts to stop him, I rashly awakened encountering a silhouette in the shape of my son, as I locked my wide eyes upon this image, I noticed it swiftly moved from the couch where I laid to the kitchen then it vanished just as suddenly as it appeared. What the hell was that? I had never seen anything like this before. I have heard of ghost sightings and other less daunting spiritual encounters, but this occurrence was all new to me. Surely this incident was the first piece of evidence that I was slowly losing my mind. Or… was I on the path to finally finding *my sanity*?

I later discovered a term associated with this type of experience. Experts refer to this as "bereavement hallucinations." Hugh Pickens explains in his essay, *Visual Hallucinations are a Normal Grief Reaction, that* this phenomenon is a normal reaction to grieving in which the mourner would see, hear, or feel the presence of the deceased. Dr. Ronald Plies, psychiatrist, suggests in *Hallucinations of Loss and*

Visions of Grief, that post-bereavement hallucinations may be part of a disordered grieving process, known as "pathological grief," "complicated grief," or "traumatic grief." Being that these types of experiences are not widely reported, there is very little evidence to support this as an actual diagnosis or syndrome and requires further investigation.

After encountering "Dewayne's apparition" or whatever *it* was, I figured I should direct my attention elsewhere as I *did not* enjoy that ordeal. Sure, I could feel him, smell him, hear him, and see him everywhere and in everything – I'd even had vivid visions and dreams of him during this time – but when the characters in the movie started to walk out of the television, I had to ring the alarm!!! Because I actually gave a damn about my sanity, even if Grief had proven He could care *less*.

Chapter 4

Grief's Heinous Matrimony

Upon the espousal of Grief and I, the shocking disbelief of the incident caused me to exhibit some very pretentious and unrealistic behavior. I presented outwardly that everything was well with my soul, that the strength of God had taken over, and that there was a level of peace that I maintained when in actuality this was a goddamn lie! I was, in fact, experiencing sickness in my soul, giving God the silent treatment, and trying to contain the burning rage inside me. I answered every single beckoning call of Grief; I was completely unaware of his possessiveness at the time. He made me think that I was in charge but truthfully, he ran the show.

Days after the incident, the perceived control factor came when I attempted to alter the situation as my chosen remedy and response to Dewayne's transition. It was painstakingly evident that my mind had escaped me as I believed I could control a situation that was incontestably beyond practical capabilities of manipulation. Spells of insanity were relieved with brief moments of stability. These spans of reprieve sanctioned mental recalibration, allowing brief moments of relief in pursuance of rational thinking. I recognized that I needed to recapture the reins of cognizance before Grief became the horse that drove this carriage into a lurid abyss. I concluded that the space and place of insanity was neither my predestination nor was it my expected end. A path that led to healing and recovery was necessary to promote growth and progression through my unwanted reality.

Although there was a monstrous intangible war waging within, when situations summoned the presence of mind, it graciously responded. As planned arrangements commenced, my mind shifted into complete business mode, which was the initial situation that called for me to be present in the moment. On the solemn Sunday, following Dewayne's sudden demise, a family meeting was scheduled. Immediate family and close friends were invited and encouraged to share ideas and offer suggestions, as I had no prior experience that afforded me to be the least bit qualified to organize an event of this magnitude.

I never imagined that I would be on this side of life, arranging funeral services for my seventeen-year-old baby. The meeting began with an appreciation speech to everyone that decided to come out and offer their support. Some family members did not choose to participate as they had speculations of foul play as it pertained to the death of my son, and instead of coming out to possibly understand a little more about the situation from one delivering known facts, they chose to deliberate elsewhere, conjuring up stories that contained only one truth, Dewayne was dead. As the meeting progressed, I explained the situation as best I could, while I tried to navigate through the swirling unanswered questions in my mind.

I decided to open the floor for questions as a tactic to buffet the production of falsities that had already begun to circulate through the rumor mill. Although it would have been an impossible feat, I attempted it anyway. Questions that had answers were answered, while others still remain a mystery until today. At one point during the meeting, I felt attacked and judged… as if I hadn't taken the proper measures to ensure the safety of *my son*. This was heart-wrenching because these attacks came from the people, I thought would undoubtedly comfort me! My wounded and bleeding heart was exposed to them as they cruelly and intentionally doused it with salt. Few seemed to care what I felt as *his mother*, as *his sole caregiver*, and *his primary protector*.

Most of the "family" that came to be "a shoulder" never visited my house, never had any special connection to *my* son, nor did they spend any significant time to *really* know Dewayne. Yet, Grief caused them to wage war with me. Ironically, they were shooting with blanks and no live ammunition. I didn't owe anyone an explanation for anything! Courteously, I shared what I knew of the situation in hopes that it would build a team of warriors; and soldiers that were equipped with truths to assist me in the battle to ward off the missiles, bombs, and bullets that I knew would come my way. Unfortunately, even in the supply of ammunition, I was often struck down by friendly fire. Although beaten, battered, and bruised, I pressed on.

Next destination on the agenda… the high school Dewayne attended. What should have been a normal slow start, academia-filled Monday for most students turned out to be one of melancholy and mourning. I decided to visit Dewayne's high school following the incident to solicit the participation of the principal and other school members in the services. Since this was Dewayne's senior year and he was on track to graduate, I wanted the services to resemble that of a commencement ceremony. I was determined not to be robbed of the graduation of my youngest child. As I sat in the waiting area inside the office, the transition bell sounded. All of a sudden, a rush of tearful students invaded the office area, some were awaiting parents to arrive to check them out for the day, others embraced and wailed together. A few of them recognized that I was Dewayne's mother and came to offer their condolences with a hug and sweet words of encouragement. There were several school psychologists present at the school to help not only the students but also some teachers cope with the loss. It was a sad day at Dunnellon High School.

As the days went by and the finishing touches were being put on the arrangements, I noticed that family participation had dwindled after the meeting. It seemed as though some of them congregated amongst themselves and discussed alternate plans without my input but would spring their ideas on me at the last minute. This was very frustrating as I was open to suggestions, but I disagreed with being completely left out of the discussions. Maybe they thought they did me a favor in an effort to lighten *my* burden; however, it had an adverse effect and just made *my* burden that much harder to bear.

During the time I needed family the most, I immensely felt the fervid absence of their vacuous presence. When it was time to decide on a church, I was given a timeline as to when things needed to be secured and I shared that with other members. The church that was initially suggested denied the request to hold the services there. That left us at square one with only a day to solidify a space. Miraculously, a church that some of my in-laws were affiliated with offered their building and services at no charge. It included everything that was needed, enough space to accommodate the prospective attendees and a space to hold recessional activities. The location was secured and finalized.

Soon after that other church suggestions came in from the others. Needless to say, the deadline had already passed, and their propositions were useless. Their recommended changes would have definitely diminished some of the things I wanted, in which the resolution was "use the church that we suggested, then the other church for the repass." This was utterly ridiculous, and I happily rejected their nonsense! I'm sure they had ill feelings, but *this decision* was MINE to make! With all that I had on my plate; I did not need any flak from anyone. Unfortunately, people are selfish and the worst behaviors manifest when Grief comes in. I received phone calls and texts from people that had never shown any concern regarding the decisions I made with my family matters, audaciously offering their opinions on how I *should* conduct things. Some even called to request or confirm that their names were mentioned in announcements and programs… Really, people? I don't know how I kept my composure.

In the midst of raining projectiles, rays of sunlight invaded the adverse atmospheric conditions causing colorful beams of light to be captured and reflected as beautiful rainbows. Friends from far and near poured out love and support with many acts of kindness. They brought food and drinks to the house, offered culinary services, donated monetary resources through Go Fund Me, Venmo, and other avenues.

They sent flowers, cards, and condolence through texts and phone calls, and some even dropped by just to sit with me. These people were the heroes that carried me through to sheltered safety as the bombs of life were detonated and released in my direction. Without them in my corner, I would have been considered a casualty of war.

Phase 3: Control

<u>Control</u>- *To exercise restraint or direction over; dominate; command.*

The arrangements were finalized, and plans were in full effect. The day of the viewing had finally come, and I did not know *how* to feel, so I decided I wouldn't and became numb. The mood that Death and Grief bring with them is an awkward but loud silence, a painful but numbing existence, and a present but absent consciousness. As we arrived at the church, my body trembled in extreme angst, a feeling that debilitated all faculties without my knowledge or consent. As I approached the corridor that led into the sanctuary, I felt a heaviness that caused my knees to buckle when all of a sudden, a warm presence was felt as if a "comforter" had descended and swaddled snuggly around my body. At that very moment, I received the strength I needed to begin my journey into the "valley of the shadow of death." I gather that the extremely short but long walk from the car to the casket in some way simulated the experience of a death row inmate that walked "the green mile" to the destination of his demise. As I reached the casket and saw Dewayne "in the box," I didn't wail like a banshee or bellow like a lion, but in a still small voice, I leaned down and whispered into my baby's cold deaf ear… "I'm gonna whoop your ass, when I see you!" Whether that statement was Grief induced or not, I meant it and it still reigns true to this day. The majesties and gatekeepers of the kingdom should verify this arrangement with the Master before my arrival so that there will be no misunderstandings when that time comes.

Announcement: Services for Dewayne Tyrell Galloway held on Saturday, May 5, 2018, at 11 am; location Kingdom Revival Church 3318 East Silver Springs Blvd, Ocala, FL 34470. That announcement delivered a deafening reticence, a blaring sullenness, which resounded in the ears of everyone who heard it. Cinco de Mayo 2018, the celebration that commemorates the Mexican Army's victory over the French Empire at the Battle of Puebla, was hijacked with a celebration that commemorated the beautiful but succinct life of my baby boy.

It was a "beautifully brilliant" Saturday; however, the circumstances behind this day were "beastfully bleak." This day was devoid of joviality and recreation, rather overflowing with mournfulness and heartbreak as we remembered one whose physical presence was suffered in absence. After many sleepless nights, I wrangled through the fatigue, the confusion, the trauma, and even the tears to vacate the cave that I tucked myself into to prepare for the day. The house was quiet and somber as everyone trudged about *ad nauseum* arrayed in the colors chosen to represent Dewayne: white paired with his favorite color, royal blue. My attire was just a little bit different. A bright yellow pantsuit accented with a royal blue jacket and suede pumps. The colors of choice were in no way an exhibition of what I felt inside: void, misery, and despair. The reactions experienced through the events were incomprehensible, inexplicable, and unfamiliar. A formidable embodiment of the infamous tale of *Ms. Found in a Bottle* as her plight through Edgar Allan Poe so eloquently inscribes "a feeling for which I have no name, has taken possession of my soul— a sensation which will admit of no analysis, to which the lessons of bygone time are inadequate, and for which I fear futurity itself will offer me no key."

The limo pulled up and we made a cheerless exit out of the house and into the car. The ride to the church seemed the longest that either of us has ever taken, me especially. When we finally arrived at the church we were met by a sea of family and friends adorned in blue and white. Although everyone appeared to be in unity and on one accord at first glance, contention lurked just beneath the surface. It was only a matter of time before the drama began. As the attendant attempted to establish order and solicit attention for structure, some family members pushed their way through the crowd to obtain a position they assumed worthy to occupy. It was an awful display of compassion. Because of all the chaos surrounding me, I could barely remain attentive to the services. Here I was preparing to walk the green mile, mount the wings of shame, and hoist the burden of guilt all the while others rehearsed for the performance of a lifetime. Yet, I persevered.

Fortunately, my church family served as a great support system along with a young lady that experienced a similar fate just a year before. Our meeting was nothing short of divine intervention. While in the midst of an "I can't breathe" moment just days before the funeral, I received this heartfelt message:

"Ms. Krystal... my heart is full for you and yours since yesterday. I cried some tears this morning from the depths of my soul for your baby boy Dewayne. I cried from my heart and spirit for you!! Many will not understand what you are going through, but my sister, I know exactly what you are going through. The waves of emotions. One moment feeling strong and the next moment feeling like you're not going to make it. How do I know?? Last year on May 24, 2017, at 7:15pm, I walked into my sixteen- year-old son's room to find that he had hung himself...I tried to save him. I tried to get him down and couldn't. I immediately felt my spirit trying to leave my body. I was ready to give up. I had forgotten that I had two small children and a husband. If it wasn't for them screaming what happened to Khalil. The gaping hole that rose inside of me was overwhelming. I was crouched over in the spirit. But God!! His grace is sufficient, and His mercy endures forever. In that moment, I felt the grace of God hold me up and said that I shall live and not die. I said all of that to say this, my sister, you hold on to God's unchanging hand. Run for him like you've never run before. There is a divine healing with your name on it.

Father God in the name of Jesus, I ask that you saturate Krystal with your spirit as she goes through this time of mourning. Hold her in your arms and allow her to rest in your bosom. Give her the peace that passes all understanding. Your word declares In Psalms 34 that you are close to the brokenhearted and save those who are crushed in spirit. In this hour where I know that you have prayed for my sister like you did for Peter, I pray that her faith will not fail her. I pray that her faith is strengthened. Burden, shame, guilt will not be her meat, but that she will take refuge in knowing that the angel you loaned her has returned to you for rest and that he is no longer in pain or suffering. Krystal, Lift up ye head o' ye gates, be ye lifted everlasting doors and the king of glory shall come in, who is this king of glory, the Lord strong and mighty, the Lord mighty in battle. In Jesus' name, I pray. Amen!!!

Be encouraged, my sister. If you ever feel like talking, please know that I am here. I will speak with you. Ask me what you want, and I'll answer you. God has strengthened me for this. And I know he will do the same for you. Job said in Job 23:10," He knows the way that I take; When He has

*tested me; I will come forth as gold…" Be ready for when God
will give you double for your trouble.*

God bless you.

The instance in which I violently gasped for air in near collapse, this epistle provided the oxygen that promoted breathing. We continued to exchange messages as that led to an invitation to the funeral, our initial meeting. The invitation was graciously accepted, and not only did she attend but she also accompanied me, my hand in her clutch as that of a doting father walking his bridled daughter down the aisle to be given in marriage. We walked in pace to the melodies of "I Can Only Imagine" as we passed between the parts and schlepped that dreaded trail together. I drew from her strength.

As I approached the metal chest that contained my lost treasure, my entire being responded to the intense weight of Grief. I peered into the chiffonier as my gaze landed upon the beautifully golden-bronzed face, pearlized smile, and statuesque physique of my baby boy. Immediately my knees weakened and buckled, my breath became short, my faculties were no longer intact. I laid my head on my son's lifeless chest as I let out the wail of a grieving mother. When the time came to say goodbye, my stare lingered just a bit longer to scan every inch of his face, I then leaned in closer as if to hear the whispers of a silent but sweet, "See you later, Ma," kissed his forehead and responded, "Okay, Son" as I took my seat.

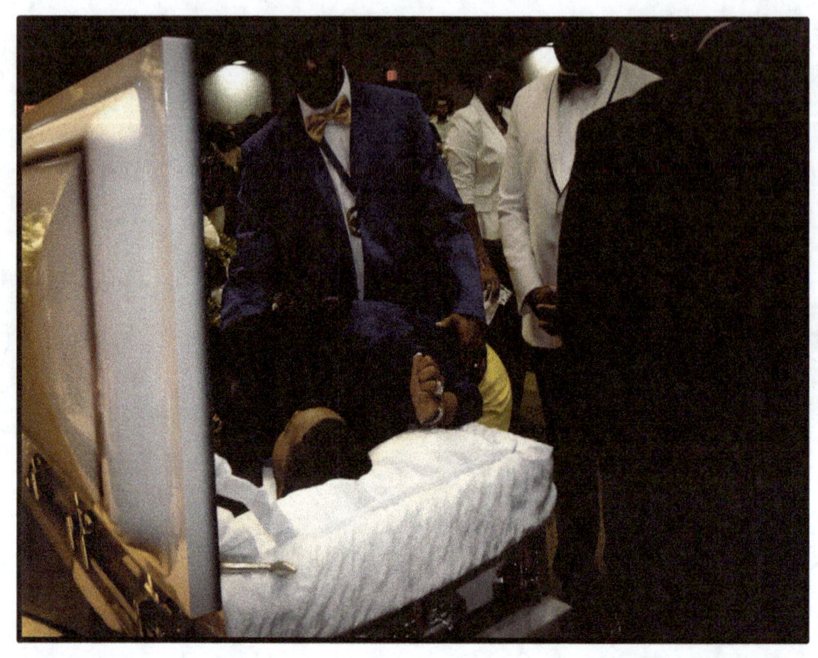

To everything, there is a season, and a time to every purpose under the heaven: A time to be born, and a time to die; (Ecc 3:1-2)

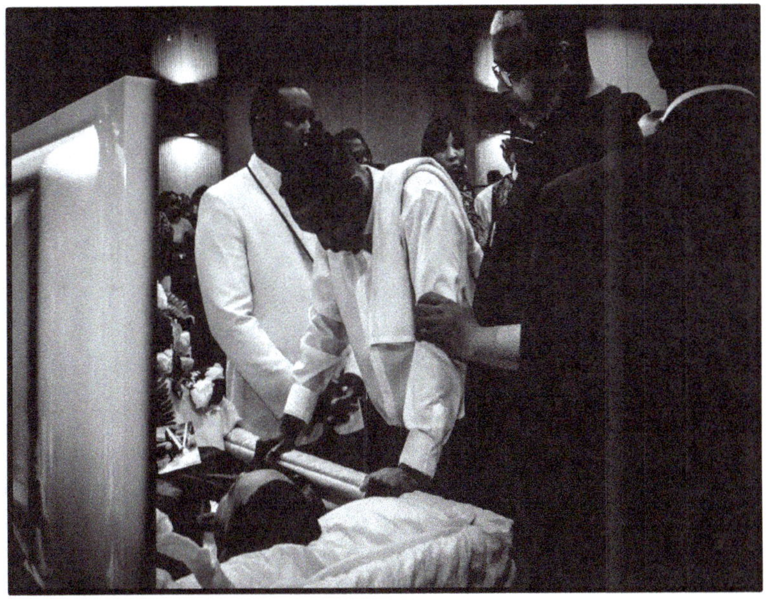

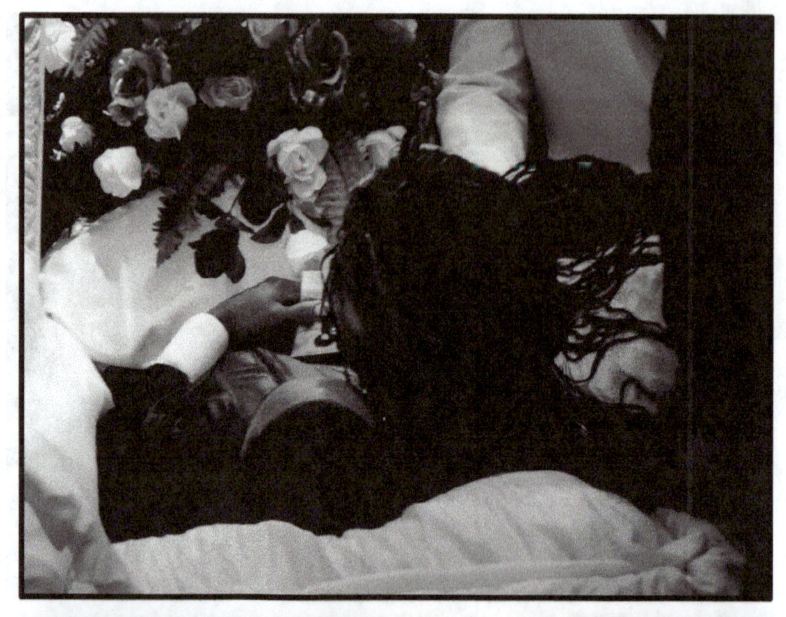

My priority at this point was to put my feelings to the side to focus on my other two children to make sure they were okay through all this. The service was beautifully coordinated although tension was high coming from "the other side." They were rude and belligerent as they expressed their disdain for the order of service and for their lack of recognition. Their attempts for disruption throughout the service were unsuccessful as the love for my son was expressed through friends, teachers, and family members as they shared heartfelt stories and special moments with Dewayne. I knew my son was special, but I had no idea the impact he had made on so many people. Keiton even mustered up enough heart to share a funny story about him and his brother. That was the highlight of the day. For him to be able to speak up at a time when he was in the most pain was huge. I was one proud momma.

This was one event that I wanted to hurry and be over and to never end all at the same time. Little did I know, "the others" shared in the same feeling of getting this show on the road as they had something much more calamitous in mind.

The announcements were made, the letters were read, the songs were sung, the diploma was presented, and the eulogy was given. The service had come to an end. We prepared for the transition, trailing the bed on wheels while we marched to the traditional graduation compilation, *Pomp, and Circumstance.* Upon approaching the exit doors, I watched as the pallbearers lifted the box in the hearse. I couldn't fully feel the effects of that moment because there were other things going on around us that seemed a bit off. I observed suspicious men in shorts and tank tops hanging around the parking lot. I felt that they were not there to offer support but to cause some type of mischief. Police were called to clear the area before anything happened. Then we were escorted to the limo to travel to Dewayne's final resting place. The ride there can be described as fast and furious as we sped to the cemetery as if we were trying to outrun the plans of the enemy. I was unable to focus on grieving as the distracting thoughts of an impending catastrophe flooded my mind.

As we pulled up to the gravesite, I noticed a car oddly parked, running idle in the middle of the field with a man standing on the outside of it with one hand concealed inside the vehicle. Immediately, my intestines begin to churn within. I had an inclination that something was about to go down. I attempted to turn my full attention to the pallbearers as they ceremonially carried my son from the hearse and placed him onto the straps that bared the weight of his steel bed and would ultimately lower him into the ground, but I felt the need to continuously observe my surroundings even in this setting. My eyes scanned the grounds in my line of vision, I noticed a family member to my left getting fidgety and moving about back and forth and other family members strategically positioned a "safe distance" from the immediate family. The final words that were spoken over my son before the committal was done with such swiftness as if the director was also aware of impending danger. As the family was dismissed, my pastors faced us to give us a warning of what we already knew: shit was about to hit the fan. No, those were not the words of my pastors but a vivid expression of what was about to happen.

Before they could move away from us, out of nowhere, one of my pastors was shoved to the ground as the raging fists targeted at my husband struck with a vengeance. And there it was just like that… an unfair fight broke out in the middle of the cement army before my son's body was laid to rest. My husband (at the time) was struck to the ground then a whole tribe of people began to pile atop of him to attempt to do him severe bodily harm. Luckily, my other son and son-in-law were there to protect him from the brunt of the beating as they attempted to "call off the dogs." All of a sudden, shots rang out and people began to scatter. My husband was escorted from the scene unscathed, and police were dispatched to clear the area. I was in even more shock and disbelief at what I was experiencing. I just begin yelling and screaming "This is not right! This is not right!" In the midst of my screams, I noticed the attendant frantically screaming. I looked up and saw my son's casket upright as it had tilted and fallen into the vault amiss. I screamed and ran over to the casket, and someone quickly moved me away. While I was being escorted back to the limo, I was met with an irate cousin throwing slanderous "bitch" slurs and making threats to beat my ass. I could feel the anger and rage welling up on the inside. I felt as though I would have been completely justified in whatever absurdity was to follow and then it happened… I filled my lungs with air and let out a strong "I'm gonna pray for you." WTF? God, Holy Spirit …really? That's all you got for such a time as this? After the smoke cleared and my baby boy had finally been laid to rest properly, I ran from the car to his grave, fell to my knees and began to belt out a fervent prayer. When the prayer was over, I returned to the vehicle and took the longest, most funereal ride to an empty house… void of family, void of friends... but laden with sorrow.

Pastors Bennie and Demetria Childs eulogize Dewayne.

Dewayne's Final Physical Resting Place

Chapter 5

Grief's Bitter Consummation

The funeral was over and while the tears of others had dried up, "I tried to keep my surface hidden as I smiled in the crowds, but while alone in my room I cried the tears of a clown." (Robinson, Wonder, Cosby 1967).

The days that followed were undoubtedly torturous. Even though love cascaded like a waterfall descending over a precipice, a faulty punctured receptacle jilted the reservation thereof. There was a hole in the bucket, Dear Liza, and there was no "one" or no "thing" that could fix it. At this point, everything was in question: my sanity, my identity, and even my existence. Full of insolence, the thrust of a fiery phallic body pierced the chalice of a vestal soul and ruptured the surfaces... As trails of blood saturated the sheets of surrender in an egregious display, Grief pompously conquered the territory… the consummation.

Now that the deal was sealed with Grief, the great divide was set in motion. Those that were supposed to be the closest to me felt the furthest away. The subsequent intrusion was not only baffling but also gut-wrenchingly painful atop the arduously existent circumstances. The headlines read as follows... BREAKING NEWS: *A particular rogue familial entity positioned as matriarch, caught in an embezzlement scandal.* Her intentions? To capitalize on the death of my son. After services had been rendered and payments settled, I learned that a certain non-profit agency had donated proceeds to cover all expenses. However, I never received the funds as they were transferred through tainted extremities. Those hands attempted to cash in on an unauthorized insurance policy in which she was the self-proclaimed beneficiary. Unfortunately, the veil was torn as the truth became evident and the funds were rescinded…

stamped: RETURN TO SENDER. This was yet another shot to the heart without breaking the skin. It was as if the shattered and scattered pieces of my quintessence were doused with a highly concentrated sulfuric acid solution, while the culprit threw the rock and hid her hand just as spectators witnessed the ghastly grotesque corrosive effects. The putrid odor of death accompanied by the malodorous stench of searing flesh, settled into the nostrils of the martyr, as it exasperated an anesthetic reaction upon inhalation… then as swiftly as she went under, she was "slapped" back into consciousness and jolted into an ongoing torture chamber in her mind.

Phase 4: Crisis

<u>Crisis</u>- *a dramatic emotional or circumstantial upheaval in a person's life*

"Someone please call 911, tell them I just been shot down and the bullets in my heart. And it's piercing through my soul; feel my body gettin' cold" ~ (Wyclef Jean).

Reality began to seep in like a slow intravenous drip of a lethal concoction. The crash of each droplet delivered flaming impulses intently and methodically like buckshot that struck center mass, hurling me into an unexplored atmosphere. Who is it that smote you? Wherefore art thou, Krystal? How did you get there? When will the smoke clear? What is this warped galaxy that you have *star* trekked into? Question after question, thought after thought, bombarded my mind day in and day out while I wandered aimlessly in a cosmic daze. I felt overwhelmingly lost as a mother, a daughter, a sister, and as a friend. Was/Am I a despicable parent? Did I deserve to be treated poorly as a daughter? What good am I as a sister? Am I friendly enough to keep friends? My mind sifted through all of the seemingly underdeveloped profiles of my life and produced nothing but negatives. In this particular darkroom, the infrared light provided was not enough to process positive images. Grief had me right where he wanted me: baffled, desolate, and marred.

I questioned my extant children on the quality of my parenting. However, they assured me that I was a good parent and that I was not the cause of my son's demise. Their reassurance helped a little; consequently, those thoughts remained constant, they even haunted me at times. In this state, I became very fearful and overprotective. I invaded my son's space by sleeping on the couch in his room to ensure that he was not alone and that this awful travesty would not happen again on my watch. I overreacted to trivial things. If I called one of my kids and they didn't answer the phone, panic would set in and I'd frantically call until I got some type of response, then I knew they were okay. To add, I would request that they notify me when they got to a place and if the timespan got too lengthy from the last time I heard from them, I would call to do a wellness check. I'm sure that was unacceptable, yet they understood my paranoia at the time and complied with my requests… for the most part.

Although I seemed to be stuck in a time warp, life continued to move at lightspeed. A number of "firsts" happened without my permission or consent. Among the "firsts" of many, I'll make mention of a few notable ones. The first hill to climb was Mother's Day. Well, isn't that an oxymoron? Here it is a day set aside to honor mothers and I'm not feeling good enough to be honored for anything. We (Keiton, Keyana, Hayden, and I) attempted to maintain our normal Mother's Day rituals. That is, church, dinner, then home. Consequently, on the ride to church, everyone was spiritless and silent as Dewayne's absence weighed heavily on our minds and hearts. All of a sudden, Hayden, my two-year-old grandson, peered into the windshield of the car as if he had some supernatural ability to look beyond the sky.

"Uncle Dewayne's in Heaven," he said, so matter of factly.

He then exclaimed, "He… he rescued him!" Astounded, we all turned our attention from the various windows that we so sulkily stared out of and looked at Hayden and then at each other. Tears filled our eyes as we clung to the words spoken from the mouth of this babe. I imagined that we were all thinking the same thing before Hayden spoke. "Did Dewayne *really* enter into heaven, given the method of his exit on earth?" At that moment I felt that our swarming question had been promptly confirmed. That very moment gave us just enough strength to get through the day.

Another notable "first" was Dewayne's actual graduation, May 25, 2018, exactly twenty days after his simulated graduation ceremony. How is this possible, Dewayne's graduation day and he was not there to walk across that stage to receive his diploma? Feeling a bit envious, I watched callously as proud parents, grandparents, aunts, uncles, cousins, and friends filled the Ocala Livestock Pavilion to take part in the ceremony that symbolized the transition from the school world to the real world. The cadence of *Pomp and Circumstance* resounded in the atmosphere as studious instructors pioneered the path to matriculation. I stood on the sidelines stifling tears as proud youngsters marched out two by two to be honored on this occasion. Even though my Dewayne had made the big transition weeks prior, in the sea of black caps and red tassels, I still searched for him only to trace him back to a still photograph on my t-shirt. My heart was heavy as the last of my three heartbeats, the mister of the ceremony, was not present to celebrate his day with us. It was truly an honor for Dunnellon High School to include him in the festivities. As parents cheered heartily for their graduating senior, we continued to listen intently for the name that was missing from the program, but not from our hearts. Then, there it was, the roll call of the absent angel: "Dewayne Tyrell Galloway." There went out a roar over the entire stadium. I cheered and sobbed and sobbed and cheered as my heart was full but empty at the same time. When the festivities were over, I walked around congratulating his closest friends and classmates. Luckily, I had a fairly large picture of my son to afford a few of his friends a photo opportunity in remembrance of him on graduation day.

Aaron and Alexis. Dewayne's friends since
Romeo Elementary

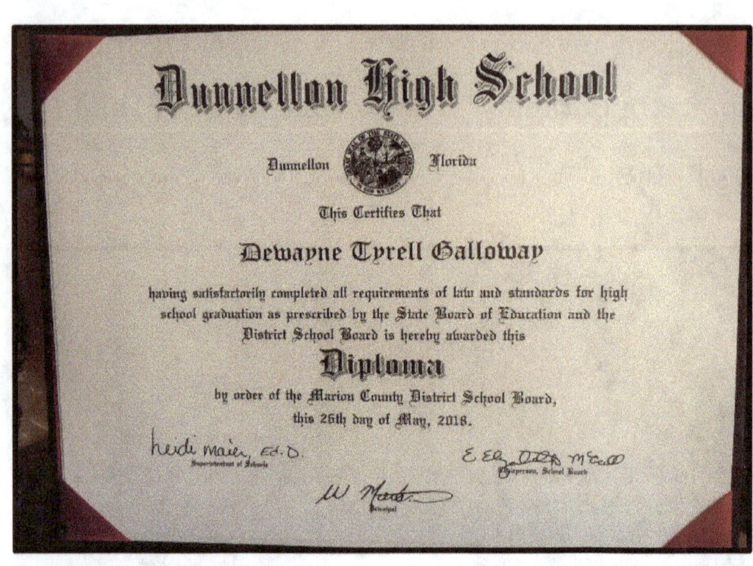

Keiton and Alexis

In any event, as far as I am concerned, all of the "firsts" were memorable; notable even. Within a year's time, a number of "firsts" without Dewayne had been experienced. Family-specific holidays such as Thanksgiving, Christmas, and New Years were especially difficult, but we managed. The final significantly emotional "first" was August 06, 2018… Dewayne's 18th birthday.

That day was extremely emotional for me as I reminisced about the life and times of Dewayne Tyrell Galloway from his birth until his death. I struggle to discern whether this was a blessing or a curse, an honor, or a dishonor to behold and usher my baby into this world, then again to behold and escort him out. From the joys welcomed in choosing a name to call him, having it documented on a certificate of birth, and forever etched in my heart; to the fears perceived hoping that his name will never be forgotten as it is called less and less, printed on a certificate of death, and engraved upon the dispassionate surface of an apathetic gravestone.

Many mothers know the progressive processes and joys in conceiving, carrying, birthing, and bonding… after giving life to a child. But only a few know the regressive processes and pains in abdicating, surrendering, burying, and detaching… after the death of their child.

Chapter 6

Unhappy "Grief-iversary"

As I began to salvage the fragmented pieces of what was left of my "normal" life; I was faced with an immense task to fashion something new, something different, and something foreign. However, I had a problem. I didn't know how to do this.

The 28th of every month had become a mile marker, a cumulative record of the days, weeks, and months since my life had totally been turned upside down and inside out. I was not ready to let my son "rest in peace."   Each day I awakened with an incurable ache in my chest; debilitating thoughts that would take my breath away and cause me to desperately gasp for air as if I had forcefully sprung up from the depths of a watery submission. Grief flooded my territory and there wasn't a "DAM" thing I could do about it.

There was nowhere I could go or nothing I could do without Grief being right there to monitor my every move. He made life so unbearable that I despised this connection. It seemed that on days that I wanted to be happy he would intentionally sabotage it and cause me to feel miserable. If I smiled, he would quickly remind me of all the reasons I shouldn't. A particular moment I recall is when my family and I went to Disney Springs. Disney is the wonderland of happiness and dreams. Up until this moment, I hadn't danced freely for several months… almost a year to be exact. Dewayne loved to dance… dancing reminds me so much of the former joy I *knew*. And on this day, Joy returned. I smiled, swayed my hips, and was in the middle of some fancy footwork… when Grief tapped me on my shoulder, and said "Ahhhh Naw, Hell Naw girl, you done up and done it. I'll be damned if you gone be happy today!" Before I knew it, I was sobbing uncontrollably but I didn't want Keke and Keiton to see me like this *again*. I walked over to a bench as if I was tired and attempted to restrain my tears. But… my kids knew, just like I knew… Grief was up to his same ole' BS as usual, and He had gotten the best of me! It seemed that my tears and befallen countenance were the fuel that kept his fire ignited. The more incapacitated I was the more empowered he became. His goal was to keep my mind imprisoned so that I could function only under his directive. Being under his control left me emaciated and appetent; however, allegorically I presented a picture of satisfaction. He nourished me with the bread of adversity and satiated my thirst with a drink mingled with my own tears. My physical and spiritual weight hung somewhere in the balance between feather and heavy. Grief was the puppet master and I the puppet. He was a narcissistic maniac that played on the empathetic strings of my heart. The irony was that this was a perfect collaboration; a perfect combination of "rhythm" and "blues."

My return to work after an extended and grievous summer was nothing short of a nightmare. I tried to bury myself in my work but every time I turned around there was some type of adversity. It all started when I was assigned to the same workplace as a certain family member of Dewayne's. In a welcome conversation with the leader of that particular place, a small segment of my story somehow found its way into the exchange. After our meeting was over, she expressed her satisfaction with my presence and that she looked forward to working with me. Well, I suppose that slight revelation sparked her recollection of conflicting events unbeknown to me at the time. The next thing I knew, I was being reassigned! <u>What the Fuck?... and Other Questions</u> by Krystal was the title that generated on my "face" book.

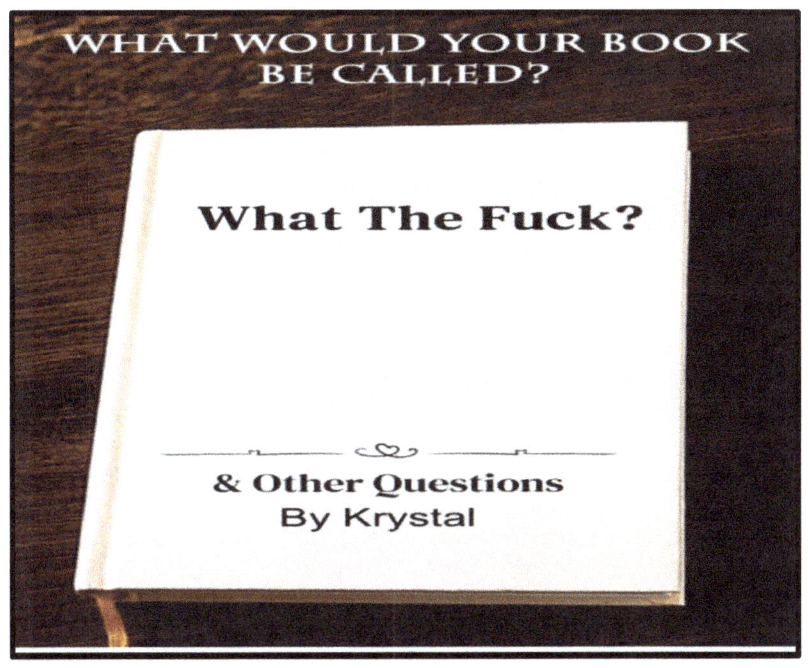

What do you mean? Why am I being reassigned? Who is responsible for this? How was this matter concluded? Of course, I was pissed, but I professionally stood my ground and made suggestions on how things should have gone. Even though my argument still ended in a reassignment I did not remain silent. Little did I or they know this was just the beginning of a break in the silence of this little lamb.

It was apparent that Grief had a squadron of snipers positioned at the ready to take me out at any moment. However, I refused to be snipped. With keen eyes and ears, I had to remain sharper than the shooters in every situation as this was the first of many assassinations attempts in the workplace. About midyear, there was another proposed reassignment. The program that was put into place at the school was not constructed properly and was failing miserably. I supposed that myself and my situation were utilized as the perfect scapegoat scenario. Lee Majors relinquished his role, I was the new fall guy on ready, "set", go.

To add insult to injury, I was mentally and emotionally tormented at work. How could I attempt to simply just live when so many aspects of my life were in turmoil? That year of my life came straight from hell [presumably]. There were losses, the divorce debacle, my 1st Angel-versary, and family betrayal. My faith was more than tested! In fact, it was almost abandoned. The unwanted shifting of my life was definitely an induction into the hall of shame, all the while I teetered on the brink of insanity.

Phase 5: Shift

Shift- to move from one place, position, or direction to another.

"It was the best of times, it was the worst of times, it was the age of wisdom, it was the age of foolishness, it was the epoch of belief, it was the epoch of incredulity, it was the season of light, it was the season of darkness, it was the spring of hope, it was the winter of despair." Charles Dickens.

This particular segment in my life was indeed *A* tall-*Tale of Two Cities*. A season of opposing views and dueling dragons brawling for supremacy; howbeit, it was up to me to decide the winner. Even though it didn't look, seem, or feel like I had much of a choice in the matter, the decision about the way to go after this travesty was mine to make. Life is a conglomerate of choices and whatever we choose has consequences whether they be good, bad, or indifferent. In my case, it was imperative for me to choose precisely, intentionally, and correctly in order for progression to occur. That was the hard part… It was so much easier to lie down and allow myself to be swallowed up in sorrow and despair than to arise and confront the situation head-on.

The very thought of a confrontation caused the earth beneath my feet to quake and resulted in pretentious and illusive landslides of failures… failures in parenting, failures in employment, failures in marriages, and failures in life itself. All in all, one thing was for certain, Grief was my constant. Even though he was an evil son of a bitch, I could always count on him to be there like a faithful, backstabbing friend who thrives on the misery of others.

After the death of my son, I was under the impression that either Sympathy and/or Compassion would have shown up when I needed them the most, but boy was I wrong. Grief's pompous ass showed up every time. He strutted his way on the scene fanning his multifaceted feathers like that of a peacock attempting to procure a mate. Instead of offering consolations, he hurled insults. He told me that I had no right to be more somber than anyone else because everyone felt the effects of Dewayne's passing? Umm… Da' fuck? (Sorry, not sorry...there is still a little ratchetness that surfaces every now and again when a certain nerve is hit). I mean I'm only his mother, *right?* How dare you say some shit like dat? This was a moment of clarity for me. In that very instant I knew that I could no longer deal with Grief in that manner. However, as cruel as that last statement was, there was yet another opportunity for further savagery. While in an intense tug of war, Grief looked me square in the eye and scoffed, "You can't leave me, it's till death do us part, baby." The minute that phrase escaped the lips of the assailant, it penetrated to the crux of the matter and caused a shifting in cerebral gears. The plan to dismiss Grief was set in motion. Infantry tactics were devised and means of combat were refined and certified.

Operation "Grief-Struck" was in full effect. I'm not sure as to why it took such an intensive degree of pain to be the vehicle that moved me from one place to the next... I guess I had a warped view of what a strong Black woman actually was. Maybe I measured strength in the number of shots to the heart I could withstand. Maybe it was a measurement of endurance or determination. Maybe my attitude about this situation was just a plain ole mashup of stubbornness and stupidity wrapped in insecurity and codependency. In any event, it was time to get my shit together... for real.

The scales had finally fallen off my eyes and the kid gloves from my hands. My perception of everything changed in an instance. It was as if the lightbulb had finally come on over my head. I concluded that I did not have to subject myself to Grief's manipulation, torture, or abuse any longer. He was taking too much from me; therefore, it was necessary to escape the magnetic force field of attraction that pulled me towards him. Once I realized the repulsive strength that lay on the opposing side, I changed the shape and orientation of my approach to Grief. The trail of tears that I was forced upon caused me to change direction and pursue a quest to reclaim stolen territory. It was time to prepare for battle. The initial order: self-confrontation, to identify and correct faulty schemes in my personal archive. In that discovery, it became necessary to stare into the darkness of my own face as it revealed the fears, the insecurities, the indiscretions, and the inadequacies that controlled me. Within the clear-sighted gaze of revelatory enlightenment, I could see that I was hiding a broken heart beneath a mask of contentment. When the *Mask* was finally *Off*, I was able to *Bare Witness* to my faulty mannerisms, ill characteristics, and shoddy decisions. It has been said that if we can "honestly identify our weaknesses by admitting what has power over us, that it allows it to become one of our greatest strengths." Conclusively, I recognized my addiction to emotional pain from toxic relationships. This epiphany allowed me to shed those ugly layers and triggered a response of an urgent change. I had to turn this thing around and I had to turn it around quickly. After the things in me had altered and shifted I was now ready to put on that armor and fight to the death. Nothing else around me or in me was going to die so I had to stand up and fight, it was either going to be me or him left standing. I can tell you one thing; it was definitely not going to be him.

Fight night soon approached and by then I was ready to face Grief. One night, I calmly looked him in the eyes.

"It's over, we're done."

In a tone of disbelief he says, "Do you really mean that?"

"Yes," I said sternly.

"Okay," he said and then continued, "If I go, I'm not coming back."

"Cool," I said.

When he figured out that I was serious, he resisted.

"I'm not going anywhere, this is my house and if anyone is going to go it's going to be you," he pompously exclaimed. Yet, I stood my ground. When there was no engagement in the war, he was trying to wage with me he became violent, still, I was not backing down, cool as a cucumber, I did not play into his emotional ploy to move me from my reclaimed territory. Once he knew that I was officially out of his grasp, he tried everything he could to intimidate me. It didn't work. Finally, he called in reinforcements to have me removed. He told them that he was afraid that I was going to do something to myself and that they needed to come to check on me. When the officer arrived, he told me what had been said and I assured him that I was fine. He gave me some advice… he said I've seen this type of scenario before and I'm gonna tell you that right after I leave you need to go to the county jail (because it was after hours) and fill out the injunction paperwork and do not come back to this house until Grief is served. I followed his directions and did just what he said. I waited until the wee hours in the morning, still no phone call to notify me that he had been served and was gone. I later found out that he would not open the door for the officers to serve him and they assumed that he was not at home. However, he was trying to avoid the inevitable, his time was up. He had to leave. I did a check at the house to make sure he was still there so he could be properly served and escorted away. When the officers came back, I let them into the house, and they directed me to remain outside while they did their duty. His excuse when they asked him why he didn't answer, he claimed to have headphones on and didn't hear. Needless to say, he got served and left with a duffle bag full of clothes and a heart full of anger and rage. He was still throwing verbal punches even while on his way out the door. He wanted so badly for me to be taken down. He even planted marijuana in my bathroom hoping that the cops will see it and take me in. However, grace is a real thing, the cops were smarter than that and they knew he put it there. From that day to this one I've been free from Grief's entanglement. Well at least from that aspect, but the residual effects of his presence remained for quite some time.

One year... touch-down! Happy Angel-versary, Dewayne…. Unhappy Grief-iversary, Krystal. Although the days leading up to the year mark had been tumultuous, I decided to pursue happiness in spite of the heartache. In the midst of an internal crisis, I would often document my thoughts, feelings, and struggles. It was seemingly the only thing that kept me afloat from the questions that flooded my mind. The focus and consistency devoted to writing resulted in the release of my first self-published literary work entitled *Bare Witness: Mask Off.* The book was released on April 27, 2019, as a testament to the mental battle that I fought daily during a period of great loss. It documented the demons encountered in the progressions of life that were presumably denounced and departed but proved to lie dormant until the perfect storm raged to bring them to the surface. It is a story of hope when all seems hopeless. That day brought boundless joy and a sense of accomplishment; however, it also brought sorrow and a sense of failure because of the colossal sacrifice it took to get there.

The next day, April 28, 2019, friends, and family gathered at "Dewayne's Curve" (a phrase coined by Hayden representing his Uncle Dewayne's graveside residence) in celebration of the life, love, and laughter he brought to everyone he met. Delightful stories and fond memories were shared as everyone fought to hold back the tears. During that time span I discovered in Dewayne's short but sweet life that he had an even greater impact than I could have imagined. Friends wrote songs, dedicated writing pieces in school publications and assignments, wore his initials on their sleeves during football games, sent shout-outs to him often on social media, and they even sent heartfelt texts to his phone occasionally. Dewayne lived and then he left; loose leaflets, single scrolled sheets of paper that told his story to the hearts of the people. Each year representing one page, he scripted a seventeen-page manual for us to read, to learn, and to grow. It didn't matter how short his album was, but what matters is the impact of his story.

After the unhappy grief-iversary date had passed, I finally stopped tracking the pain month-to-month as one would with the progression of a baby after their birth. I knew that I still had a long road of recovery ahead and was reluctantly willing to take the trip because I had no idea what lay ahead. I wanted to live again and somehow, I knew that if I were to continue the course, resurrection would be just around Dewayne's curve.

Hayden holds a picture of his beloved "Uncle DEWAYNE"

Photo credit: Shot by Sam

Chapter 7

Thin Lines Between Love, Grief, *and Insanity*

"Grief, I've learned, is really just love. It's all the love you want to give but cannot. All of that unspent love gathers in the corners of your eyes, the lump in your throat, and in the hollow part of your chest. Grief is just love with no place to go."

~Jamie Anderson

**<u>WARNING</u>: The following chapter is intended for mature audiences and contains Adult Content, Graphic Language, Explicit/Offensive Material, Unmasking, Bare Witnessing, and Strong Emotional Content… Reader's Discretion is Advised.
(I woke up like this! ~Beyonce).**

In learning, language, and literature there are a plethora of lines to reference. Lines of symmetry, lines of latitude, lines of longitude, lines of communication, intersecting lines, parallel lines, vertical lines,

105

horizontal lines, crossed lines, blurred lines, disconnected lines, phone lines, thin lines, lifelines, and flat lines… just to name a few. In my experiences with said lines, I've crossed a few, blurred a few more, paralleled some, and flat-out disconnected others.

My entire life, since the dawning of my conscious memory, has seemed to be a compilation of blurred lines and misses. Misadventures, mishaps, misappropriations, and misunderstandings. Here's a little background information to get the gist of my tyranny. I grew up in the church. When someone makes this type of statement it usually alludes to them having a strong moral foundation. Well, let me just say that is a bunch of malarkey and that's putting it nicely. I know plenty of people (I am people) that "have grown up in the church" who have moral compasses that are busted, crippled, cracked, jacked, and wracked. To have grown up in church was not an osmosis experience where someone absorbs morality by attending ritualistic services at least once a week, it simply means that they attended church so much that it was basically a home away from home. Time spent at church equated to the same amount of time, if not more, as time spent at home. This place called church was the epitome of a one-stop-shop. It offered a multitude of products, goods, and services to its members, all under one roof, so to speak. If you wanted to be entertained, the melodic ensemble was there to meet the needs of all who wanted to lend an ear. Later, the production company of the entertainment committee added solo performances; liturgical dancing, miming, poetry slams, and the occasional show of talent by a random pew sitter who was moved by the spirit and ran center aisle to show off the hip hop moves he or she had been practicing for the Sunday occasion. If it was counseling you needed, there was an opportunity for group or individual sessions. Group sessions were scheduled on Sundays after the entertainment portion. It began with the reading of scriptures from one we informally call the "speaker of the hour," formally the Reverend or Pastor. He or, in some cases, she would read excerpts from the "Good Book" and attempt to explain to everyone why they are not living up to what is written. Oftentimes, they (the Reverend/Pastor) are not, in fact, living up to those teachings that they so passionately preached about, but simply presenting themselves to be a picture-perfect living epistle. The individual sessions included confidential, one-on-one time with said Pastor/Reverend for the purpose of expressing woes, trials, tribulations, shortcomings, downfalls, and imperfections with the hope of receiving wise counsel. However, when reconvening with the group, you find that the confidential information that was shared in that private setting somehow makes its way into public demonstrations as the topic of the Sunday Sermon. I believe the term "putting it on blast" was coined after the occurrence of this type of experience in the church. If it was a dining experience that you wished, you stuck around after a special program or funeral. The mothers of the church would fill your plates with full course meals that surely satiated your taste buds with delectable goodness. These churches also offered opportunities for charity. They collected money for and from the ill and incapacitated, better known as the "sick and shut in," for building expansions, and for various mission excursions. Fundraising was a specialty as well, they hosted the sale of candy apples, baked goods, spaghetti dinners, chicken dinners, rib dinners, and the infamous fish fry. Some places offered other goods and services that consisted of the purchase of a special word and accompanied by the laying on of the hands by persons with special gifting called Prophets. They would make an interest request for people that were willing to give a specified dollar amount. For example, they would make a $100 request, then everyone who was interested in exchanging the $100 for a chance at a special word and a touch from that individual would stand up, form a line, and wait their turn while the audience looked on in amazement and envy that they could not afford to take advantage of that rare opportunity. Hospitality was huge in the church. At the end of every service, visitors were invited to join their family by exercising the open-door policy. If interested, you would take a stroll to the front of the church and prop yourself in the chair that was set aside for this event, and they welcomed you in with prayer and hugs. Occasionally, there would be an overnight stay at the building that consisted of all-night prayer with something called "tarrying." I never really understood what that meant and to tell you the truth, I still don't.

I've been to many churches, and I've seen and heard many things. My grandmother was big on church, and I accompanied her to what seemed like every church and every church service there was. We attended Baptist, Pentecostal, AME, Methodist… YOU NAME IT! I was CHURCHED. Sadly, the only thing that years of attending these services taught me was that I needed to attend because that's where God was when we needed Him to either get or keep us out of trouble. There was no real understanding of an established relationship with God. After years of clocking into these services Sunday after Sunday, I felt like God and myself had gotten very well acquainted. I've gone through the typical life struggles, and the not-so-typical ones- molestation, abuse, domestic situations, things of that nature; all of which I felt I overcame through what I knew about God at the time, and I considered myself stronger because of it.

My life was not the best, but it was manageable, tolerable even, and God and I were on relatable terms. There was the occasional call to him on the main line to tell Him what I wanted. However, He never came through exactly when I wanted him, but he was always on time and that was enough for me. I was conditioned to go through hardships, this conditioning is owed to the church. Week after week of Sunday services were full of stories of tragedy and triumph as they continuously went through hardships but were miraculously delivered from them all. It was funny how these people never had a break; something was always going wrong in their lives. Of course, they attributed it to the Devil's work. As you know he is always busy and never takes time off. The saying was if the Devil was not working against you then you were working with him. The protocol to all things was prayer-- telling God what you wanted and letting him work it out for you. It seemed like simple instructions to follow. Just pray, hold my peace, and let the Lord fight my battles then victory shall be mine; I could do that. That was the creed that I patterned my entire life after. That method presumably worked for me… until one day it didn't. Then, in came Grief with his funky ass on April 28, 2018, and completely changed the game.

My world from that point on was forever rocked. That day came with a rush of feelings, pangs, and emotions that I can't even name or describe. It was as if I had entered into a time warp and everything around me moved in such swiftness, but I was suspended in both physical and mental succession. That single event had me questioning my very existence. It challenged the relationship *I thought I had with God.* Another "What the Fuck?" questioning moment arose as I thought, "God, I thought we were good. What in the hell is going on right now?" In a state of shock, disbelief, and confusion, I defaulted to the strategies and coping mechanisms that I'd previously learned and utilized to carry me through tough situations. Although this trauma superseded anything that I had ever experienced, I attempted those methods to no avail. This was not supposed to be my battle. If that were true, then why was I wounded beyond measure. As soon as I felt the pain from the battle wound, I quickly withdrew from the conflict.

Being void of emotion, I suffered from disillusionment, exhaustion, isolation, and imposter syndrome… Krystal had left the building. I would talk about my situation as if it was some type of spiritual heroic odyssey. I didn't know how to feel this, I didn't want to feel this, but attributed the facade to strength given to me by the God of the "church that I grew up in." This was the perfect opportunity to give the performance of a lifetime. I must say that it was quite the act. I wrote the script, starred in it, directed, and produced it. Oh yes! I was the Great Pretender... Church Attender.

Phase 6- Existing

<u>*Existing*</u>*- being in a specified place under certain conditions*

Have you ever been in a headspace in which it was extremely hard to function, hard to get out of the bed, hard to do practically anything? Not the average superficial pettiness that we often make reservations for a pity party of one or throw rainy day parades for those self-inflicted sorrowful situations. I'm referring to the real deal, no fault of your own, helpless, and hopeless inside a massacre that can't be seen with the naked eye. At first glance, a healthy, whole, and happy individual appears before you, but a careful examination in an ultrasonic view detects profuse internal bleeding from areas that weren't even known to exist.

Losing a child is the most excruciatingly painful event that I believe one can experience in this life. It's cruel, inexplicable, tormenting, confusing, unfair, and simply just fucked all the way up. There are no manuals, no books, no pamphlets, no journals, or other literature that offer any sufficient information or comfort to that experience. There aren't any carefully constructed intellectual deliberations or cleverly combined pulchritudinous words that were or are enough to ease the pain, the tension, and the torment.

I would often muse over tales of grieving mothers before me. I've studied the faces of those mothers during their bereavement. At that time, I was on the side of, "I can't even imagine what you're feeling right now." Their faces told a story that my heart could not conceive. I could only offer sincere condolences and allow my heart to go out to them, but only for a moment. Then upon its return, the lubb dupp sounds of normal sinus rhythm sustained. Now, after sitting in the place of a grieving mother, I understand those stories. I understand their faces. My heart grieves with their hearts. My heart had failed just as the hearts of mourning mothers before me. Normal sinus rhythms were interrupted by the piercing snap, crackle, pop sounds of an incessantly broken heart.

I was afflicted to the point of death. I needed a lifeline before I flatlined. My lifeline existed in knowing the Lord is close to the brokenhearted. I was and am brokenhearted. I am still on life support. During the processes of introspection, the shedding of layers ultimately exposed the rottenness of my core. My thoughts revealed that my grief was not my only problem. It was at this point; I became offended by the rancid stench of decomposed flesh that jolted my senses and caused a conscious awakening of ME. Out of this awareness, I became more vigilant. I sought out strategies for support, I needed answers, I needed understanding, but more importantly, I finally realized the purpose of Grief was to truthfully expose ME to ME.

I began to take inventory of my life, my decisions, and my foundation. The first thing under review was my faith and upbringing in the church. Sure, Biblical principles are foundational greats, but only when there is understanding. As a matter of fact, when my churched faith was tested, it failed miserably and so did I. According to Romans 10:17 ESV, "Faith comes from hearing, and hearing through the word of God." Let me just say that at some point in this process I blocked my hearing both internally and externally in silent protest against what I was going through. I did not want to hear anyone's words.

In my analysis, I concluded that I had treated the church like a pharmacy that prescribed highly addictive mood-altering and temporarily stabilizing drugs. They worked until I could no longer get a higher potency. I was all "churched-out!" I felt there was nothing else "the church" could do for me… so I asked, "God do you hear me, do you see me, but most of all do you FEEL me?"

His answer was a resounding YES, although visually and not audibly. I heard Him with my eyes and saw Him with my ears. In other words, I saw what God was saying. Eventually, I recognized that when God rescued Dewayne from mortal agony, I was summoned to reconcile the torment within my own life. No more Bebe bandages, no more Gucci gauzes, and no more superficial stitches. I had to put down my Michael Kors crutches. I stopped bullshitting with God, came to him in all my ratchet nakedness, and I told Him how the fuck I felt. It wasn't pretty. It wasn't supposed to be. All false fronts were removed, displaying the ugliness in me. Ironically, it was a freeing experience! And in that experience, I began to loosen the grip of postmortem rigidity in the gradual release of the beautiful urn that held Dewayne's ashes [figuratively speaking] God allowed me to see and experience the beauty of his life and not dwell on the sadness of his death. Grief couldn't control me anymore as I decided to allow God to set me on a straight street to prepare me to dwell in a city called BEAUTY-FULL.

When I realized the brilliance and the artistry that awaited my arrival, I learned and understood that we can't just pray the ugly things away, because ALL of it works for our good. In our misunderstandings, I think we've become accustomed to the "Just go to God and drop things in His ear" and expect Him to *just* work it out, to *just* do it, Lord, and JUST fix it, Jesus!

Well, He already said it was finished and we have the burden of the greater works. The Bible says faith without works is dead. I believe this is how it works. I go to God in prayer and that looks like conversation, asking, reasoning, petitioning. Stemming from prayer, I receive information, answers to my questions, strategies for my dilemma, and solutions to my petitions. All of those things come with acts. I have to put into action the information that I received through prayer. Which has led to more mature prayers and conversations where thanks, praise, reverence, or what we may consider "worship'" is incorporated along with or in place of the asking, reasoning, and petitioning so we do not feel condemned by our humanness.

Chapter 8

Overcoming the Entanglement of Grief

"Nothing in life will call upon us to be more courageous than facing the fact that it ends. But wisdom is on the other side of heartbreak."

(Movie: Wish You Were Here, 1995)

My entanglement with Grief definitely took me on a journey that almost led to the point of no return. The twists and turns, ups and downs induced roller-coaster effects of anxiousness, panic, and fear. In my lack of control, I attempted to manipulate my environment to create a sense of morbid serenity. Little did I know that these events would cause further entrapment in the forceful boughs of Grief's embrace. Desperate pursuits to posthumously imprison my dearly departed dependent produced vivid impressions of reality through "enshrinement' or "shrining." In *The Grief Recovery Handbook,* James and Friedman describe enshrinement in its most damaging form as obsessively building memorials to the person who has died. Let me just tell you that I was the queen of enshrinement. I put my creativity to work and built a mini-museum filled with Dewayne artifacts. His room was a monument of epic proportions. His bed was draped with a blanket displaying photos of great memories, his dresser still filled with the clothes he had so neatly folded. Perched on the top of the dresser sat his brush and doo rag. His nightstand was staged with his cheerleader uniform with the shoes displayed at the side. In the closet, hung his best shirts and pants. Lastly, in the corner of the room on the floor by the half-filled laundry basket, lay the clothes that he wore on that last day of school.

The shrine even extended throughout the house. A rustic accent cabinet was purchased to house precious keepsakes. A graduation cap encased in a shadow box rests atop the cabinet surrounded by a collection of golden crowns. Large pictures and paintings of him were hung on various walls and a memorial wreath positioned at the front door greeted all who crossed the threshold. To top it off, there was an engraved cross placed in the exact spot where I found him outside. Not to mention, secretly tucked away was the blood-tinged white sheet that covered him on that dreadful day. I admit, my collection of memorabilia was both sacred and sinister. My biggest fear, although I know that it could never be possible, was forgetting him. Having to continue in this life without him just seemed so wrong. I did what I felt I had to do to keep him alive not only in my heart but also in my home.

At some point, I knew that harboring all these things was not healthy for me as it not only brought great memories, but it also generated a perpetual stream of bad ones. However, I was comfortable in the temple which contained the altars I had erected. One day, a still small voice, call it consciousness or what have you, chided the noxious activity and instructed me to tear down the contemporary mausoleum, noting that if I were to keep it in place that there would be no forward movement and further hinder productivity in my mind, my heart, and in my life overall. Of course, this revelation was upsetting as if I hadn't been through enough, now there is even more work to do. I felt a sense of entitlement; I had the right to hold on to my son by any means necessary. Wasn't it enough that he was taken from me in the worst way? Now, I was required to let go of more of him. I wasn't feeling that at all. Consequently, the tormenting activity that plagued my mind caused me to reevaluate the situation. That mentalistic encounter brought the realization that even though I was chosen as the door that would allow Dewayne to pass through from the spiritual realm to the earthly one, there was another keeper of the door to allow passage from the earthly realm to the spiritual one. And at that door, I had no jurisdiction. I realized that you can indeed love something and still give it back. Needless to say, the sanctuary was dismantled, and London Bridge came falling down. Cleaning up the debris after destruction seemed to be more tedious than the initial duties. It became just that much harder to let go. Cleaning out his room was THE hardest thing ever. As a matter of fact, I had to bring in reinforcement as I could not carry out the mission alone. When I tried to do it, my emotions got the best of me. I had an overwhelming feeling that I was throwing pieces of him away. Lord knows that was the last thing that I wanted to do as I felt in a sense that I had failed him in some way.

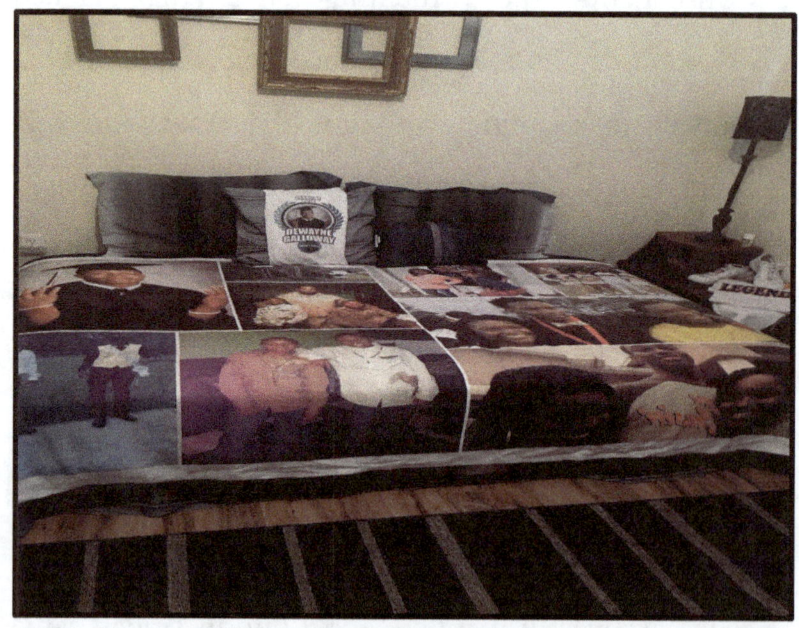

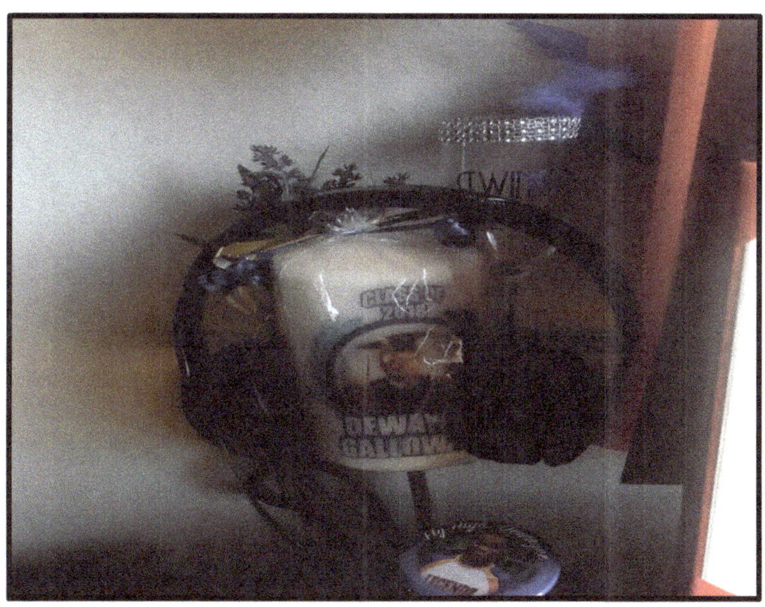

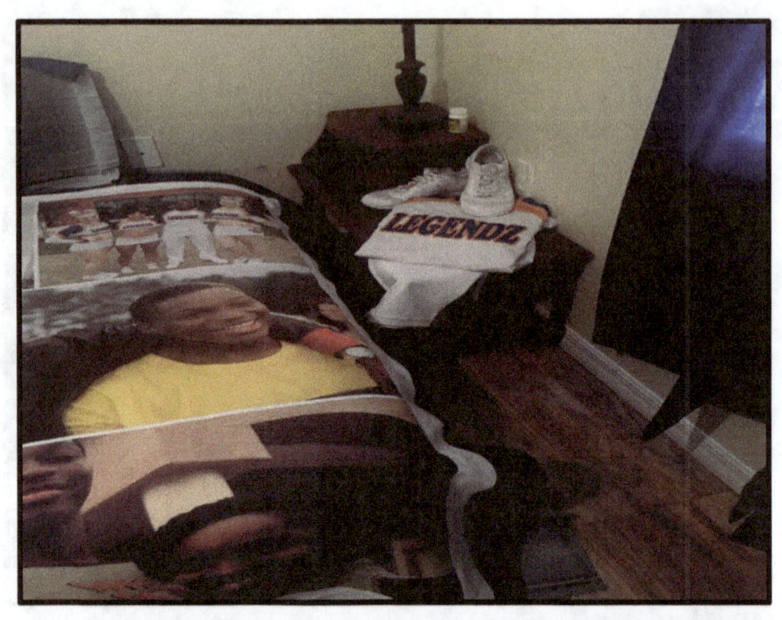

LEGENDZ

2018

When I finally accepted the guilt from the extra mile that I didn't take, I was able to forgive and release myself from the harnesses of Grief and thus release my baby to peaceful stillness.

Phase 7: Grieving and Healing

Grieving- *deep and poignant distress caused by or as if by bereavement.*

Healing- *to make well again: to restore to; to cause (an undesirable condition) to be overcome MEND*

Grief had definitely done a number on me and affected every facet of my life. In addition to the emotional response to loss, Grief also had physical, cognitive, behavioral, social, cultural, spiritual, and philosophical dimensions. All of which I needed assistance in understanding and coping. Some friends and acquaintances, who were childless, were quick to offer condolences and advice that could in no way assuage the intensity of my pain because they could not in ANY WAY relate to what I was experiencing. Although their efforts were genuine, their rationale was completely inadequate for my situation. Case and point, we cannot attempt to help in situations that we have not been in ourselves, because no matter how spiritual or educated we may be some things we simply must go through to understand. And even then, logic still seems to escape us.

Should you or a loved one find yourself in the middle of the abyss of Grief like me, don't attempt to articulate it, don't attempt to over-spiritualize it, the best thing to do is to allow yourself to feel it. There is no specific timetable for grief, so please do not let anyone persuade you to attempt to speed up the process because they feel you should be "over it" by now. Everyone goes through their own processes in the timing necessary for them. Allow yourself time to move at a pace set for you. Just because you seem to be moving at a faster rate doesn't mean you're more productive and a slower pace doesn't indicate less productivity.

If you are a supporter, most times it's better to allow the bereaved time to sit with their Grief and be there as a shoulder for them to cry on when they buckle under the immense weight. Simply allow yourself to be present in the turbulent and not so turbulent moments with them. This is what helped me, there were people who loved me, took care of me, and they never took my distance, my lashing out, or my semblant insanity personally - they simply stayed with me until Grief released his demonstrative overpowering grip; and for that I say thank you and I love you always!

Fortunately, I have a friend that is a true God-send! She is a Certified Grief Recovery Specialist. She provided clarity for what Grief is and more importantly, how the "stages of grief" were initially formulated for those who were suffering from a terminal illness. This helped me to understand that my approach to dealing with Grief was warped because I was not battling an incurable ailment. Although, I felt like I was. This was yet another epiphany. Consequently, this revelation allowed me to realize I didn't have to acclimate my recovery to my misinformed intelligence.

The counseling sessions we experienced together were not like typical counseling sessions. The healing process required me to address my fears, my shortcomings, my faults, and most importantly the parts of me that made the Grieving process comfortable and unbearably discomforting simultaneously. The honesty I had to have with myself, oftentimes petrified me and at other times the honesty was liberating. Within my personal acknowledgment of self, the things I had done as well as the things that had been done to me, I was able to see how my life had been ruminations of hurts. She helped me to see that I could change my reflection to an image that I loved! When I did this, my healing began to surface authentically! I was able to remove yet another mask, the one of false healing, and it uncovered the paths of genuine healing in which I can now tread lightly. I recovered the things that I had lost in childhood traumas, relational traumas, career traumas, and so much more. I worked tediously to understand how I had inhibited my own healing, and once I got out of myself and faced myself, healing became available and attainable.

Finally, I was able to relinquish my parental rights and allow THE FATHER to reclaim custody. I said to God, "He is ALL yours... *again*." I remembered that God is the ultimate keeper and there were no greater hands to be placed in than His. The letter addressed to my baby boy Dewayne reveals my ascension from Grief's watery grave to Healing's restorative palace. Now, I earnestly understand that out of the end of a thing comes the beginning. Thus, better is the end of a thing than the beginning.

Hey Dewayne,

It's been a while since I've seen your face or heard your voice other than the occasional videos or pictures I often look back on. I miss you dearly and oh what I wouldn't give to have you back with us. I'm sure there is nothing that you're missing with your bird's eye view of everything, but there is so much that we're gonna miss with you. We're gonna miss first and foremost that beautiful smile, your sense of humor, your playful ways, your over-exaggeration, and dramatic antics. Those things were/are you. But there are other things we're gonna miss. Kenyan's, Keiton's, and Hayden's future babies are gonna miss their Uncle Dewayne, we're gonna miss your first car, your wedding, our mother son dance, your first house, your first child, I could go on forever. I know what these first two years were like without you, they were pure hell. I can't bear to project to the future and try to think how the days are gonna go then. I would probably drive myself crazy with worry and stress, so instead,

I'll continue to take it moment by moment, day by day, week by week, month by month, and year by year.

I apologize that I didn't recognize the signs, that I didn't go deep enough into our conversations, that I didn't just let you talk without trying to fix it. That I was easily agitated after a while. I'm sorry that I missed it. I forgive you for leaving the way you did; my heart was and still is a little broken but I'm healing. I was never mad at you, I just didn't understand, and I still don't, but remember what I said to you at the church.... I meant that, I'm still gonna beat your ass when I see you, so be ready to wear one.

As I reflect over this entire situation, I can't discern if it's all a blessing or a curse. For a mother to see and usher her son into the world to lead and guide him to the best of her ability in the way he should go. Then to see him transitioning into the next life with a knowing that she poured all that she had into them for the time that she had them. To receive such a great gift, then to return it back to the giver. The Bible does say that favor is deceitful. That statement has definitely proven true in this experience. I have definitely learned A LOT, but the greatest thing I've lear+ned is that I have a vast capacity to love. That territory was enlarged if nothing else. I love you past death and beyond this world. I didn't even know that was possible. There have been numerous things that I've experienced in these past two years that I didn't think were possible both good and bad. I am still blessed beyond measure. I am saddened that your life was cut short but am very appreciative of the time I had with you. You were and still are a light that glows in my path. I love you, son. Keep my seat warm for me. Until we meet again... so long, see ya later, adios, bon voyage, arrivederci, goodbye for now

Love you always and forever,

Ma

Chapter 9

The Learning Curve on the Road to Recovery

"Grief has important lessons to teach those who pay attention"- Harold Ivan Smith A December Grief

The Krystal-line Effect

Clear as Krystal

Welcome to our journey!

Allow me to re-introduce myself, today I am a follower of Christ, however before this transformation took place in my life, I would've been known as Sparkle and Ice.

Know that everything that glitters, or rather sparkles, isn't gold, so let me tell you that you've been warned or better, yet you've now been told.

I was a blend of many different things, active ingredients, if you will. A little bit of this and a whole lot of that…so your best bet, if you didn't know, was to keep your ass back!

With the hurt and pain that I felt from the rejection, an ice-cold attitude became my flow so yeah, I searched for love in all the wrong places and found promiscuity instead while living my life at subzero…but frankly speaking, I became a sub-zer-hoe!

I went by the name of Krissy you see, and there were days that I wondered if she was, she or am I me? Either way, the behavior exhibited was definitely that of a pre-Christ Krissy, again living a life that lacked identity.

So, trying to make sense out of her nonsense would be insensible; to her, her logic was undeniably right; therefore, she tried repeatedly to satiate her emptiness with a heart that was cold like a block of sparkling ice.

My journey continues…however this time around, I know who I am, due to an encounter with thee I Am that I Am. I became a beautiful work of art as the Master began to chip away at the block of ice that surrounded my heart, a flawed piece of clay, sculpted into what you now see today. I stand before you completely free because yes, she was, she and I now know me!

Being exposed by His light, everything in me finally being revealed; that brokenness, those bruises I could no longer conceal, and honestly, I was tired of trying to hide what really needed to be healed.

Yes! I was a little bit of this and a whole lot of that…finally surrendering my life to Christ and He gave me life back. Now I thank you for your time, as you read or listened to a snippet of my life in a spoken word rhyme. My transparency has been vulnerable, allowing others to see into me, and yet I have no fear…because there were days, I thought that I was clear as Krystal, since being in Christ,

I AM KRYSTAL CLEAR!

<u>Krystal-in- Effect</u>

Written by Tonya Edwards

Sparkling ice or Follower of Christ. Which one were you? Which one are you? Which one will you be? I am Krystal but was once known as Krissy. God has called my name twice to pull me up from where I was or to where I am supposed to be. It wasn't that I didn't understand who I was, not that I don't know who I am, the problem was that I didn't understand who God intended me to be. I was just being who I thought I was, I am just being who I currently am, but I am always preparing for who I am DESTINED to be. This is the Krystal-line effect. What path would I choose; would I be iced out or Christed out? The initial option seems much less complex as it involves the least amount of know-how, thought, or preparation. However, when those underdeveloped strategies are applied, the deception of perception is that it is beneficial and works for our own good, but in the end, is utterly meaningless. In contrast, the latter option is rather tedious and requires knowledge, wisdom, and understanding to be procured then applied appropriately to trials, situations, and circumstances. This allows spirit and nature to align to create a balance of perfection or maturity.

I have learned that trials are opportunities that come to build or make us IF we are willing to learn the lessons in them. Situations are presented to develop our minds to strategize what we have learned in the trial. My creative play on the word "sit-u-a-tion" means that "u- sit and develop an action." It is then and only then that your situation has the potential to change because you planned to change it. Even in that, knowing what to do is not enough. Knowing is only half the battle; the other half is applying what you know. Then there are circumstances that are proposed to establish fortitude; a sense of strength in well-roundedness, if you will. Everyone has heard the saying "what goes around comes around;" without regard, we casually insert this phrase when referring to karma coming back to check someone for a wrong, they have done. I tend to think this phrase has a much deeper interpretation and is aligned with the scriptural reference (Ecclesiastes 1:9, NIV), "what has been, will be again, what has been done will be done again; there is nothing new under the sun. With this in mind, our circum-stances (**circum**- to go around; **stance**-a mental or emotional position adopted with respect to something) are things that have already happened; therefore, have already been dealt with in some capacity. So, when a particular thing comes around again, we can execute what we learned in our trial and our situation to defeat our circumstances. If we fail to take advantage of the learning opportunities or diminish the value in development amidst the presentation of trials, situations, and circumstances we tend to repeat the same ignorant responses. The funny thing is that we still expect favorable change… (Insane much?)

I both detest and cherish the purifying melting pot into which I was placed. Naturally, it hurt like hell, burning a Dewayne-sized hole that consumed every fiber of my very being. Spiritually, it was refreshing as the purifying fires tore through my dwelling destroying everything that did not resemble or reflect health, wholeness, and purity. I believe it was much like the fiery furnace that the Hebrew boys experienced. The fire was three times as hot as anything I could have thought or imagined. However, it was in that place that I saw the Son of Man. In the midst of the blaze, I was both crucified and comforted, I was confronted, yet cultivated. Ultimately, I was convinced and converted.

The frigid, dry ice that encapsulated my soul kept me cold and away from the heat that was meant to burn away the impurities. Frozen in time is where I was at rest.... relying on the ice to numb the pain of the breaks, the bruises, and the contusions I've suffered and tried so hard to conceal. When fire met ice, I could no longer maintain my tough and gelid exterior. The consuming fire burned away every false fact that I believed about myself and charred every page in the script of the convoluted doctrine that religion had taught me. The puddle of water that was left calmed the raging fires and became my baptismal reservoir even though I almost drowned in it. The fire and the healing waters, although brutal, proved to be beneficial. Now, Krystal is what Krystal does, sparkles and exudes the multiplicities of color in every facet of her prismatic being.

Phase 8: Dying and Living

Dying- _gradually ceasing to exist or function; in decline and about to disappear; occurring at or connected with the time that someone dies._

Living- _the condition of being alive._

"It's bigger than us" is a phrase I often uttered to my son as life got in the way of our plans and attempted to ruin our purpose. This adage was meant as encouragement to keep going, to keep fighting, and to keep believing that we mattered and, in the end, we will appreciate the tough times that carved out the minuscule intricacies of every hook and nook of the puzzle pieces that neatly fit, joined together in the big picture. Little did I know that this phrase that he adopted as his own, would be the mantra that I would have to live by after he was gone.

"Sometimes what the good Lord has to teach us comes in ways we don't see." (Witches, 2020) Although, the film referenced is considered a depiction of art as life… I felt that certain segments of it captured portions of my own existence in an incomprehensible form of abstract art. I could not reconcile with God or myself that "my" baby boy was supposed to die before me. I experienced a mind-fuck and heartbreak simultaneously, but I was taught to believe that we accept what God allows. But the catastrophic and unfathomable nightmare of losing Dewayne was not a moment to rationalize with God calmly and quietly in a still small voice. Instead, I screamed, "WTF, God why? Is this really your motherfucking plan? What is the GOD-DAMN purpose in this, what am I supposed to see?" And

God replied, "Me." Now this simple reply was that in which I was left to ponder. I had plans, but there was another plan in operation. It didn't matter how much I protested the injustices or unfairness. It didn't matter how much I pleaded my case or objected to your honor. The judgment call was overruled and sustained. That single moment in time marked the sentencing of execution by a high voltage electric shock that led to my demise.

My induction into the after-life... life-after Dewayne; was a dual rebirthing experience. At the time of his birth, I was a 22-year-old mother of two children. The pangs of contractions and dilations caused an eruption in my inner parts and resulted in a release of life. Adjustments and alterations were made to accommodate the expansion as this bantling was acclimated into the family. At the time of his death, I was a forty-year-old mother of two remaining children. The anguish of constriction and elision caused lacerations to my vascular organ as a result of his departure. Readjustments and mending were performed to suture the cavernous vacuity that remained after the extraction. As morbid as the situation surrounding his death was or is there were and are LESSONS to be learned. We just have to sift through all of the ashes and debris to find the hidden treasure. It is not an easy race to run, nor is it a straight road to travel. There are numerous curves, uneven pavements, and soft shoulders along the way. Nonetheless, it builds endurance, stamina, and fortitude if you persevere as "the marathon continues" (Nipsey Hussle).

In a book of poems entitled *You're Not a Girl in a Movie,* Hala Alyan passionately expresses that "a thing does not have to feel good to be saving your life." This thoughtfully constructed phrase clearly flows from the heart of someone who not only understands pains but also understands the value of the lessons learned through them. Every person will embark upon some type of pain in this life, but not everyone will appreciate the expense of the acquisition of knowledge, wisdom, and understanding in it or through it. The enabling experience along with precious time will be wasted on repeated problematic cycles that should have long ago been settled. Time is the one thing that we are completely oblivious of how much of it we actually have. It is irreplaceable and non-compensatory, meaning once it's gone there is absolutely *NO- thing* you can do to get it back.

Life has a plethora of courses to attend and extensive lesson plans to implement. Consequently, death is inevitably embedded into the coursework. It is strategically placed on the timeline of life marking the end of one thing, yet mystically symbolizing the beginning of another. Unfortunately, during the Spring 2018 registration period, my schedule defaulted to class HRT-0428. There was no alternative course to replace it, there was no means to drop it, and there was no refund on the exchange for it. It was necessary that I go through it to engage in the required readings, complete every assignment, pass every test, and learn every objective that was presented. In that course, I learned how to live. Each one of us is given a measure of riches to steward over. Among those riches is time. I conclude that no matter how much of it we have we should spend it wisely and not wastefully. Just as the tangibleness of money is valued and managed by counting it, saving it, and budgeting it; the intangibleness of time should be valued and managed in the same way. However, if you have not mastered the one it is impossible to even fathom the other. And yet if there is still time, therein lies opportunities to learn. I apply the value and managing system to every aspect of my life. This causes me to fully embrace who I am and to be *just as I am;* to love without reservations, to forgive without reflection, and to encourage without reprehension. As a borrowed excerpt of John Green in his novel <u>The Fault in Our Stars</u> simply states "there are infinite numbers between 0 and 1. There's .1 and .12 and .112 and an infinite collection of others. Of course, there is a greater infinite set of numbers, between 0 and 2, and the list goes on. Some infinities are much vaster than others." There are days, many of them, when I resent the size of my unbound set. I want more numbers than I am likely to get, and God, I wanted more numbers for Dewayne Galloway than he got. But Dewayne, my beloved son, I cannot tell you how thankful I am for our little infinity. You gave me a forever within the numbered days in your seventeen "short" years and for that, I am eternally grateful.

Chapter 10

Reminiscing Happily… Grieving Progressively

"Fully engaging in mourning means that you will be a different person from the one you were before you began."

- Anne Brener, Mourning and Mitzvah

"Just be sure to notice the collateral beauty. It's the profound connection to everything."

- Collateral Beauty, 2016

Death is heavy and daunting. Life is light and jubilant. Recently, I experienced both at the same damn time. In the midst of my progressive healing process, my mother passed away. Initially, the pain of my mother's passing didn't affect me the same way as the death of my baby boy. It was different, our relationship had been somewhat estranged most of my life, but we were finally getting to a place of purposeful reconciliation. Then she was gone, the possibility for us to have the mother/daughter relationship I yearned for was snatched away from me, and death was the mocking culprit of my disappointment and pain. I will never know if she shared my desires, and I can only hope that our final interactions were an indication of that. Fatefully, her death occurred twenty days shy of the anniversary of Dewayne's transition. I cannot stand Death's inevitably frustrating and unfathomably attentive ass!

Soothingly, two days before my mother's light dimmed into eternity, a new light emerged, she illuminated my path and gave me hope! Haelyn Dee Grace Miller is the light my world needed to know that God is the Giver of all Givers. When I realized that my granddaughter's life was and is the embodiment of God's love, I realized that Grief could not steal the joy I find in her existence. Amazingly, I am able to recognize the grace of God in all of this. Although it is not easy, my life feels as confusing as a damn rat maze right now, I understand that if God strengthened me to be where I am now, He has ultimately equipped me for where I am purposed to be.

Cynthia Loretta Carr
10/10/1960 - 04/08/2021

The constant push and pull of Life and Death as they simultaneously exist creates a tug of war. The perpetual teetering back and forth is enough to break down the strongest man or woman. The battle of Life and Death is unavoidable. Sometimes it seems easier just to let go of the rope and take the "L," and face defeat. However, God won't allow us to fold that easily EVER! Miraculously, we get a second wind and the sweet and gentle blow by the Holy Spirit as He arises and encourages us and lets us know He's there. We grip a little tighter, dig our feet in a little deeper, and pull a little bit harder. Tired, sweaty, browbeaten, bruised and calloused we experience victory and that feeling my friend is what makes it all worthwhile. Death receives another TKO and God proves nothing is more powerful than Him!

Life and Death are constantly placed before us. When one shows up the other is ever-present. It's our choice, the decision is left at our discretion. Our initial choice is what is appealing to the eye, then it's what makes us feel good and important, and finally, it's what we think will "put us on" or gives us status, bragging rights. "Lust of the eyes, lust of the flesh, and the pride of life" is Death's strategy and he calculates it very well. Life is just that; it takes information, intelligence, and implementation or more simply stated, knowledge, wisdom, and understanding, and all of this is realized in Life and Death.

When Life and Death stand together, we do not have an innate ability to just choose life. We have a direction, a suggestion, a hint that that is indeed the way to go. The process takes a little longer but is well worth it. As Life and Death stand before me with their best presentation Death looks more appealing as it is so elegantly adorned, subtly flashy, and tactfully tethered. While Life is plain and simple: no-frills, no feels. It is what it is. We have to take in ALL of it. However, Death tastes good at first bite, sweet, savory, and succulent. It feels good going down and is addictively blinding. It creates an illusion that "I got it all together" and for that, I'll work hard to keep this image/imagination going. Life, however, is bitter and flavorless, but beneficial and healthy. Death is haughty and proud. It wants to be considered prestigious, powerful, and placid. Life is meek and humble. It does not want to be considered, it wants to be chosen, it wants to just... Be. Death looks like the better package, the better choice but in the end, it is multiplied ... death times two. Life is indeed the better choice as it is never-ending, bringing with it exuberant joy in abundance.

Each one of us has our own personal struggles to overcome. It will always be one thing or another. A forever fight to the DEATH of something. If it's your season of boxing, just know that if you are a child of God you're already trained and conditioned for this, use your skills; just know that it is up to you to determine how many rounds you're gonna go with this. You can T.K.O. in the first round or you can pitty-pat, bob and use your weave, take a few punches, get tired, worn, swollen, beat, battered, and bruised going all twelve rounds. It's your choice to make and that is one thing no one can really help you with …CHOICE. "You can get with this, or you can get with that," and of course, the choice is yours (Black Sheep, 1995).

I fully understood the continuity of death after Dewayne's celestial matriculation. His transition meant I had to reposition EVERYTHING. I wondered, "Who rearranges their entire existence in the middle of their life?" That to me is the real definition of a mid-life crisis. God responded, "I created life and I've defeated death, Krystal. I don't rearrange, I simply arrange, restore, rejuvenate, and rehabilitate when it's necessary. Dewayne has been rescued and restored and it's time for you to be rehabilitated." In the words of Chadwick Boseman, The Black Panther (Our Forever Black Superhero), "In my culture death is not the end." So, I now understand Death doesn't have the same grip it used to have because I now realize He has always been dead… I am alive and Death is envious of the Life I embody and the Life I still have the ability to produce.

Phase 9: Growing/Resurrection

Growing- undergoing natural development by increasing in size and changing physically; becoming greater over a period of time; increasing.

Resurrection- the revitalization or revival of something. The ability to rise again.

To everything, there is a season, and a time to every purpose under heaven: A time to be born and a time to die; a time to plant, and a time to pluck up that which is planted (Ecclesiastes 3:1-2). Dewayne Tyrell Galloway and Cynthia Loretta Carr have had their time of birth, but they have also been certified in death which included exit strategy agreements not requiring my consent.

Their seventeen and sixty years under heaven may have been short-lived by our calculations, leaving behind a warped perception of incomplete aspirations and unfinished legacies; however, it was just enough time to fulfill the purposes that they accepted by

GOD. The lives that they lived, the light that emanated from them was immeasurable and each impacted their own individual planetoid. Even in the silence of death, permanent products of their existence speak volumes as the voices of their lives reverberate a lasting echo within the hearts of the people they encountered.

Dewaynes
Little Sister
August 6th 20
April 28th 20

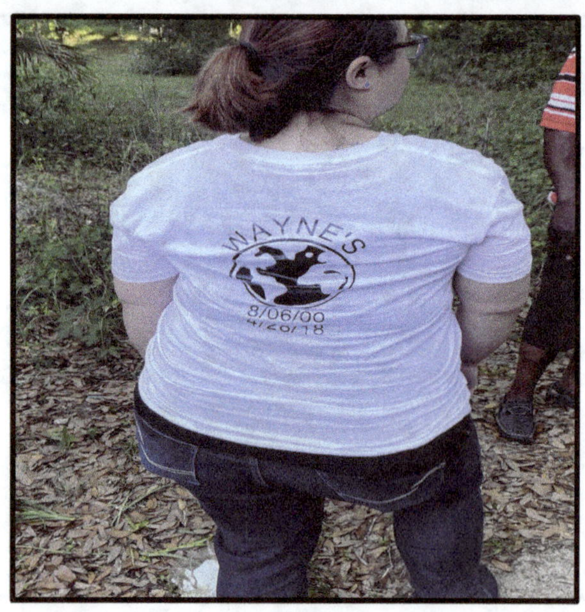
WAYNE'S
8/06/00
4/28/18

Beloved Son
DEWAYNE TY
GALLOW
AUG. 6.
2000

DEWAYNE
GALLOWAY

With both my baby boy, "Dee," and my mother, "Cymp" I was handed the unfortunate task to stare deeply into the pitiless face of DEATH. Having to close the door to the life that I brought into the world, then to do the same, just shy of three years later, to the one that brought me into this world were the hardest and most painful tasks I've ever had to complete. Ironically, closing these doors allowed openings to others. Sovereignly, the doors of heaven were opened to them both as they joined the cloud of witnesses and were added to my personal cheering section from the skybox as I continue to play this game of life.

Dewayne's afflictive fleeting ultimately made way for wondrous things to come fluttering into my life. His death caused a rearranging in the air's molecules that made the atmosphere excessively heavy. Grief straddled across my chest like a demon in the night, making it hard for me to move or even breathe. Within that struggle, I lost all consciousness, lost the ability to use my faculties, and lost all rhythms, beats, and sounds of life. I died… flatlined. I died to a facade, an identity that I had created and worked overtime to maintain, that created the illusion (if only in my mind) that I had it all together. I died to religion, a practice of rituals that kept my mind contained in a vault, restricted my movement, and diminished my productivity. I died to myself, to every aversive situation that caused me to think I was unworthy of happiness; to every abusive fist that was raised against me in protest of my individuality and uniqueness; and to every ill word spoken to me, over me, around me, and behind my back…to that, I gave up the ghost and I was the sole attendee of *that* funeral.

At the very moment the *son* darkened; the earth shook, the rocks split, and the tomb broke open as the veil was torn in two. A new me was resurrected, one that was unrecognizable to those that formerly knew *ME*. The *Son* had set me free, and I was free indeed. From the seed (my seed) that died and was planted in the ground grew a great tree. Fortitude was the reward of sowing sacrificially, watering in tears, and allowing the Son/sun to permeate the friable soil.

This tree began to bear and bare witness to good fruit. Fruit whose aromatic fragrance attracted symphonic honeybees instead of pestilent fruit flies. Love was in the air. Not the fermenting fallacy of faux pas love, but the reality and truthfulness of pure, unadulterated L.O.V.E.

I never knew what real love in a relationship was until the path was cleared for Vincent, my knight in shining armor, to meet me at the window of my cave. He loves me like I have never been loved before and this love allowed me to let down my hair to allow him access into my palace. To share the world with him changed everything. Once I was changed and learned to love myself as God loves me, my "flaws and all" were embraced as the fingerprints of my existence. I was and still am a work in progress, an under-construction mess after demolition. Subsequently, the clearing of the land, the fortification of the foundation, and the engineering design of updated blueprints will eventually lead to the production of the boldest, towering, and alluring structure to be admired, even from afar.

In a state of incompleteness, he loved me and called me his (because I accepted). I believe the love he expresses towards me is a vivid depiction of how Christ loved the church as He gave himself for it. In my ups and out my downs he loved me through it all. On days that I thought he couldn't understand the magnitude of my pain, I penned a reminder love letter:

To my Sweet Vincent Rhea "Babyface" Sancho,

I love you with all of my heart. You are the most loving, caring, generous, attentive, self-less, adoring king on the face of this planet. I am so blessed that I am your wife, and YOU are MY husband. The past few weeks have been kind of a wave for us, not that there is something that either of us is doing wrong, but our rhythm is a bit off. We're hearing two distinct types of music in our heads. At some point "our" song started to skip, and my Pandora defaulted to an old familiar hymn while yours continued to play.

As I anxiously wait for my song to play out, I noticed that you were feeling the frustrating effects of the lyrics. I know you don't understand why the song has to continue when the solution would be a simple fast forward or swipe to the left, but the truth is it has to play to the **v**ery end, some days even on repeat.

As this unfavorable song of my heart runs its course, I still manage to consider your heart even while mine is breaking. During certain times, the volume is "all the way turnt up" and won't "turn down for what." With this unpleasant sound constantly ringing in my ears, I scream inside myself over the music, and you receive it as a whisper…. Please Vince, just be patient, the playlist will shuffle soon, and we will be back moving and grooving in no time. You don't know, nor will you ever understand the pain of a mother's heart after the death of a beloved child.

There are times when words don't equate to what I feel inside and therefore cannot be expressed or communicated verbally but released only through tears. When these times occur, I need you to know it is okay to have the same LP playing in *the background. It's okay not to have identical playlists, but when my song plays just watch me as I do my dance and do your best to feel the music as my entire being responds as the beat goes on. Unfortunately, this song may be played more frequently as it is a fairly new release and cycles through quite often. When the tempo slows and the mood is solace, don't get discouraged. This song only lasts for a moment in comparison to the rest of the playlist… Our songs will play again and play often as we take full advantage of those priceless moments of life, love, and laughter.*

So, Vince, if you would please… learn to sit and listen to the quiet storm and sway with me until the next track begins; because at this moment this particular song is what my heart has to perform. I love you!

Love always and forever,

Your Wife

Since "He" has cleared the buildup of plagues that once constricted circulation to the anterior ventricles of my heart, Love now has the ability to flow freely. Relationships that were once estranged have been restored and renewed as I have been blessed with the ability to empathize without reservation, discern without conviction, and forgive without concession. The expansion has overtaken my heart, my mind, my soul, and not to mention my ass. *Did she just say, 'her ass'?* Yes, she did...lol. Happiness has also caused a growth spurt in my physique. This miraculously spread, which the D&C Diva Dynamic Sister Duo calls the *"Bae, let's go get something to eat,"* took me from a sopping 125 lbs. to a droughty 160 lbs. This takes the scripture "to whom much is given, much is required" to a whole other level. It is now required that I spend some time in the gym trying to manage, shape, and redefine all this "much" that has been given to me. Truth is, I wouldn't trade it for the world.

It's amazing how much a little seed can produce in such a short amount of time given the right nutrients. I'm not sure what this newly planted seed will produce, but I'm sure it's gonna be BIG (Pastor Mike Jr., BIG 2019).

"*Your pain is the breaking of the shell that encloses your understanding.*

Even as the stone of the fruit must break, that its heart may stand in the sun, so must you know pain.

And could you keep your heart in wonder at the daily miracles of your life, your pain would not seem less wondrous than your joy.

And you would accept the seasons of your heart, even as you have always accepted the seasons that pass over your fields.

And you would watch with serenity through the winters of your grief.

Much of your pain is self-chosen.

It is the bitter potion by which the physician within you heals your sick self.

Therefore, trust the physician, and drink his remedy in silence and tranquility:

For his hand, though heavy and hard, is guided by the tender hand of the Unseen,

And the cup he brings, though it burns your lips, has been fashioned of the clay which the Potter has moistened with His own sacred tears."

Excerpt from The Prophet

By Khalil Gibran

"Nothing's ever really dead if you look at it right"

(Collateral Beauty, 2016).

Every opening is a corridor of escape, a doorway to both exit and to enter. Branches or limbs provide a hoist that goes beyond our reach, positioned towards heaven to allow us to climb out of our misery and stand above our situations. So, let's just grow [purposely] beyond the grief.

About the Author

Krystal Carr is simply a small-town girl living in this lively world. A world in which life doesn't necessarily go as planned. Consequently, it will take us by surprise. This concept has proven to be the bane glory of her existence; beginning with her accidental, but God purposed service within public education. Krystal received her Masters' Degree in Educational Leadership from Saint Leo University. She has served behaviorally challenged students as a professional educator for nearly two decades.

Krystal has now authored her second literary work, *Bare Witness II: Growing Beyond Grief*, she takes her readers on a raw and vulnerable journey of self-rediscovery while living and growing beyond the grieving stages of her life.

Krystal loves all things beautiful, exquisite, and undeniably distinct. So, in her spare time she enjoys interior designing, traveling, and reading.

www.ingramcontent.com/pod-product-compliance
Lightning Source LLC
Chambersburg PA
CBHW071514140726
47997CB00005B/1968